PEKING MAN

Cao Yu
Peking Man

Translated by Leslie Nai-Kwai Lo
with Don Cohn and Michelle Vosper

Columbia University Press/UNESCO
New York   1986

UNESCO COLLECTION OF REPRESENTATIVE WORKS
CHINESE SERIES

This book has been accepted in the Chinese Series of the Trans-
lations Collection of the United Nations Educational, Scientific,
and Cultural Organization (UNESCO).

Columbia University Press
New York   Guildford, Surrey
Copyright © 1986 Columbia University Press
All rights reserved

Photographs copyright © 1980 Peter Krupenye;
reproduced by permission.

Printed in the United States of America

Library of Congress Cataloging in Publication Data

Ts'ao Yü.
    Peking man.

    Translation of: Pei-ching jen.
    I. Lo, Leslie Nai-Kwai. II. Cohn, Don.
III. Vosper, Michelle. IV. Title.
PL2815.A8P413 1986   895.1'25   85–16626
ISBN 0–231–05656–7

Contents

Translator's Note	vii
Cast List	ix
Dramatis Personae	xiii
Act One	1
Act Two	85
Act Three	125
Scene One	125
Scene Two	160
Photo insert	77

Translator's Note

Traditionally in China all drama was lyrical. Early in the twentieth century, Western-style "spoken drama" (or *huaju*) appeared on the stage for the first time. But it seemed that the new dramatic movement, unable to compete with the more established traditional opera and the increasingly popular movie industry, would become yet another futile attempt by progressive dramatists who epitomized the spirit of changing times.

In the 1930s Cao Yu emerged as the savior of the movement: his *Thunderstorm* (1934), *Sunrise* (1936), and *Wilderness* (1937) won him instant fame and success, as well as the hearts of the Chinese people. From then on, "spoken drama" had a permanent place in Chinese culture.

In 1940, Cao Yu wrote *Peking Man*, considered by many as his masterpiece. The play depicts the decline of a once-prominent scholar-official family in China. With piercing insight, Cao Yu unmasks the tensions and hypocrisy inherent in Chinese polite society, exposing with contemptuous humor and guarded optimism the clash between traditional Chinese gentility and modern humanitarian ideals.

Peking Man brilliantly mines the richness and subtlety of the Chinese language. It was our labor to interpret Cao Yu's art and adapt it to the English language. We encountered many difficulties. At times we adhered strictly to the original text; at other times we felt it necessary to allow our creative instincts and imagination to guide us through the translation of Chinese terms for which we were unable to find acceptable English equivalents. At all times we were aware that this particular translation would serve as a script for a stage performance. The present translation is based on a revised version of the play, published by the Renmin wenxue chubanshe (People's Literary Press) in 1954. In the original version published in 1940, the "Peking Man" is actually personified in the role of a gigantic worker whose bone structure is being studied by an anthropologist living in the Zeng residence. The playwright himself has confided that he preferred the symbolic portrayal of the "Peking Man" to the awkward superimposition of a Herculean character on stage.

While translating *Peking Man*, we were always in awe of Cao Yu's meticulous descriptions of his characters and settings, as well as his ability to penetrate the souls of his characters. Yet Cao Yu writes with grace and ease; the reader is captivated by the force of this seasoned storyteller. In moments of frustration, when we were haunted by our inadequacies, we would refresh ourselves by admiring his talent for expressing ideas in such simple yet poignant and profound language.

Michelle Vosper collaborated on the translation of act 1; Don Cohn on acts 2 and 3. It has been an education for us all.

L.L.
Hong Kong

This version of *Peking Man* was first presented in New York City at the Horace Mann Theatre, Teachers College, Columbia University, on March 25, 1980, with the following cast:

ZENG HAO	Peter Yoshida
ZENG WENQING	Isao Sato
ZENG SIYI	Lori Tan Chinn
ZENG WENCAI	Kim Miyori
JIANG TAI	Freddy Mao
ZENG TING	Keenan Kei Shimizu
ZENG RUIZHEN	Ginny Yang
SUFANG	Kitty Mei-Mei Chen
CHEN NAIMA	Mary Mon Toy
XIAO ZHUER	Willy Corpus
ZHANG SHUN	Jae Woo Lee
YUAN RENGAN	Henry Yuk
YUAN YUAN	Marcia Uriu
THE COLLECTORS	Addison Lau and Philip Soo Hoo
POLICEMAN	Philip Soo Hoo

Directed by Kent Paul
Production designed by Quentin Thomas
Produced for Columbia University by Andrew B. Harris

PRESENTED BY THE CENTER FOR UNITED STATES–CHINA ARTS EXCHANGE, COLUMBIA UNIVERSITY, IN ASSOCIATION WITH THE CENTER FOR THEATRE STUDIES, COLUMBIA UNIVERSITY.

Dramatis Personae

ZENG HAO (HAO, sometimes called "Old Master"), the old patriarch of an old family residing in Peking; 63 years old.

ZENG WENQING (WENQING, sometimes called "Young Master" by Chen), Zeng Hao's oldest son; 36 years old.

ZENG SIYI (SIYI, sometimes called "Da Nainai"), Wenqing's wife, Zeng Hao's daughter-in-law; 38 years old.

ZENG WENCAI (WENCAI, sometimes called "Gu Nainai" or "Gu Xiaojie"), Zeng Hao's daughter; 32 years old.

JIANG TAI (JIANG, sometimes called "Gu Laoye"), Wencai's husband, Zeng Hao's son-in-law, who formerly studied abroad; 37 years old.

ZENG TING (TING), the son of Wenqing and Siyi; 17 years old.

ZENG RUIZHEN (RUIZHEN), Ting's wife, Zeng Hao's granddaughter-in-law; 18 years old.

SUFANG (SUFANG, sometimes called "Su Meimei"), Zeng Hao's niece (the daughter of his wife's sister); 30 years old.

CHEN NAIMA (CHEN, sometimes called "Chen Nainai"), Zeng Wenqing's former wet-nurse; around 60 years old.

XIAO ZHUER (XIAO), Chen Naima's grandson; 15 years old.

ZHANG SHUN (ZHANG), a servant of the Zeng family; around 30 years old.

YUAN RENGAN (MR. YUAN), an anthropologist; 38 years old.

YUAN YUAN (YUAN), Yuan Rengan's only daughter; 16 years old.

COLLECTORS A, B, and C.

POLICEMAN.

Scenarios

Act 1. The day of Midautumn Festival—in the parlor of the Zeng family, Peking, China.

Act 2. About eleven o'clock that night—in the parlor of the Zeng family.

Act 3. Still in the same parlor.

> Scene 1. Approximately a month after act 1, at dusk.
>
> Scene 2. About five o'clock the next morning, before dawn.

Act 1

It is almost noon in Peking on the day of the Midautumn Festival.[1] The scene takes place in the small parlor of the Zeng family, over which a gloomy silence hovers. There is no one in the parlor; one hears only the ticking of the old Suzhou clock on a long table along the right wall of the room, with its hesitant, enfeebled tap-tapping steps. Outside, the flock of pigeons that the master of the house raises is circling in the air. Every now and then, one hears the cool hissing of the bamboo whistles tied to the pigeons' legs,[2] a sound that is loud and pleasing. Framed in the row of well-washed windows along the rear of the living room are tufts of clouds floating aimlessly in the clear blue sky.

This parlor serves as a foyer for the living room and the bedrooms of the eastern wing of the house. There are four entrances to the parlor. The door on the right leads to the bedroom of Da Nainai.[3] It is covered by an exquisite jade-green curtain of the finest gauze. The door on the left leads to the bedroom of Gu Nainai,[4] Zeng Wencai. There is no curtain covering this door. The door frame is smaller and dirtier, sug-

---

[1]The fifteenth day of the eighth lunar month, specially set apart for the worship of the moon. In the evening, families usually gather under the glow of lanterns to enjoy mooncakes and other festival specialties while gazing at the moon. The gathering can take place in the gardens, on the roofs, or in the ancestral halls. The festival has taken on many names, among which are the Harvest Moon Festival and the Feast of Lanterns.

[2]During a conversation with the playwright, the translator learned that it was a common habit of Peking residents of old to tie small bamboo whistles to the legs of pigeons in order to induce pleasing, musical sounds while the birds were in flight.

[3]A respectful way of addressing the mistress of the household (here, Siyi).

[4]A respectful way of addressing a married daughter of the patriarch of a family (here, Wencai).

gesting that the decor inside that room is also less elegant. Two-thirds of the back wall of the parlor is a folding door, curtained in blue satin, which leads into the living room. It serves as a side entrance to the living room. The remaining part of the back wall is partitioned by a bookcase that forms a small study cove. Separating the parlor and the living room at the base of the threshold is a stone ledge that one must step over in order to enter the living room.[5] Through the opened folding doors one can see the living room, which has an air of elegance revealing that this family was at one time powerful and wealthy. The main entrance off the living room is on the right-hand side, and opens wide onto a courtyard where one can see date trees, wisteria, and aspens. Sunlight is pouring into the living room through the row of sparkling windows. Above the entrance to the partitioned study is a placard bearing the three Chinese characters, "Yang Xin Zhai,"[6] written in seal script style.[7] On the left-hand side of the study is a small door (which can hardly be seen). This door leads to the backyard and into Old Master Zeng's bedroom. Along the wall of the study are rows of book cabinets filled with books bound in the traditional Chinese style. In front of the window is an elegant cedar desk and teakwood stool. On top of the desk are writing instruments—brushes, ink, a grinder—and some exquisite porcelain ware and curios. The masters of the household would come here to compose poetry and paint. At times they would come here to read the Classics, to discuss religion and philosophy, to cast fortunes, or simply to take naps.

The parlor was formerly the place used for private conversations. When the Zeng family was at its peak, the house was often graced by important guests. At that time [Great-grandfather] Jingde Gong, the founder of this once-powerful family, had established a rule: only close relatives and friends would be invited into this parlor. Decades later, the parlor has remained a place for the Zeng family members to congregate. Now, the mistress of the house, Da Nainai (Jingde Gong's

---

[5]These ledges are usually about ten inches high.

[6]"Studio of Cultivation of the Mind."

[7]Ancient-style Chinese characters.

granddaughter-in-law) lives with her husband in the bedroom on the right-hand side. Thus domestic matters are discussed only in this parlor. Though the family's financial decline has made it necessary for them to rent out the living room and western bedroom[8] to an anthropologist, the Zengs are unwilling to relinquish this part of the house. It is the last shelter for the Zeng family.

The decor of the house is maintained so as to serve as a reminder of the glory of yesteryear, and veils the family's financial misfortune. The octagonal window looking into Da Nainai's bedroom is still highly polished.[9] Behind the window are heavy apricot-colored curtains. Da Nainai is a secretive person who would never permit anyone to see what she is doing in her bedroom, and one perceives that innumerable secrets are locked away inside. In front of the clock in the parlor is a jade "ru yi"[10] wrapped in gold-threaded brocade. This scepter has been passed down from their ancestors. Placed on either side of the scepter are pots of orchids, and a pair of ruby-colored antique vases that were a part of Da Nainai's dowry twenty years ago.

In front of the long table is a square redwood table that looks a bit old and chipped and is covered by a purple tablecloth. At mealtimes this table is pulled out and converted into a dining table. On the table is a big bowl of sweet candied fruits. Around the table are two or three chairs and a low stool, all of which have been carefully polished. Along the left-hand wall of the parlor and near the entrance to Gu Nainai's bedroom is a sandalwood table in the shape of a half moon. On the table is a bowl of bergamots,[11] several snuff bottles wrapped in green satin, and a few books of the Classics. In the middle of the table is a transparent fish tank with several goldfish swimming peacefully among the seaweed. In front of the sandalwood table are some small sofas and one low end table. On the left-hand wall is a scroll of calligraphy of cursive script

---

[8]The western bedroom cannot be seen by the audience.

[9]In the old-style mansions in Peking, there were often indoor windows between rooms.

[10]A "ru yi" is a scepter that expresses "fulfillment of wishes," or "happiness."

[11]A kind of citrus fruit tapered on one end.

written by Dong Qichang.[12] *The mounting is old but elegant. On the wall near the corner of the study hangs a seven-stringed lute in an elegant holder made of orange brocade, with a tassle hanging from it. A beautiful painting of bamboo composed in graceful but vigorous ink strokes hangs on the wall between the study and the folding panels of the living room. The mounting still looks quite new. To the right of the painting is a lamp which hangs from a five-foot black ebony lamp-stand carved in the form of a dragon. The dragon's mouth is clenching a silk shade. The four-sided lamp shade is made of silk on which colorful birds and flowers are painted. By the left-hand side of the painting is a wide-mouthed white porcelain urn with blue flowers. This imitation Ming antique contains more than ten scrolls of paintings. Next to the urn are two small, square stools on which a slightly opened leather suitcase has been placed.*

The room is quiet, and outside one hears the intermittent whistling of the pigeons in flight. It seems that in the long lane outside someone, with great effort, is pulling a single-wheeled water cart, a vehicle unique to Peking in those days. Rolling along the uneven cobblestone surface, the cart makes a monotonous sound, "zhu-niu-niu, zhu-niu-niu." Occasionally the gloomy silence is also broken by the sound of a "knife-sharpening" hawker who blows a battered trumpet.

A few moments pass.

From a distance, the Da Nainai of the Zeng family and the servant Zhang Shun enter hurriedly from the door of the living room that leads to the courtyard, and through the living room into the parlor. Zhang Shun, a Peking servant about thirty years old, follows respectfully but worriedly behind Da Nainai.

Zeng Siyi (which is Da Nainai's name) was born and raised in a family of wealthy scholars. She is proud that she is educated and knows well the etiquette that is a way of life in a family like the Zengs'. She is clever, sophisticated, and wears a lingering smile on her face at all times. Yet she is also pretentious, selfish, loquacious, and suspicious.

[12]Dong Qichang (1555–1636) was a prominent calligrapher who lived during the Ming dynasty.

She considers herself a generous and gracious person, but in fact she is calculating and conniving. She envelops herself in an aura of secrecy within which she plots and schemes. In her speech and mannerisms, she always displays the virtues expected of a good wife in a feudal society and therefore appears to be kind, filial, and loving.

She is a woman of small stature with rabbit-like eyes that are slightly slanted. She has a wide forehead, a straight nose, thick lips, and buck teeth. Her dark, heavy eyebrows are penciled neatly and severely into the form of two blades. Always alert, she steals glances at others to detect their facial expressions while she speaks. Although under forty, she is overweight and has a puffy face. Wearing a pale yellow "qi pao"[13] *dress in a floral print and a pair of gold satin shoes, she enters with a stack of bills in one hand and a chain of glittering keys tied under her arm.*

ZHANG *(smiling):* What do you think should be done, Da Nainai?
SIYI *(pouting):* Ask them to wait in the hallway.
ZHANG: But they said the bill had to be paid right now.
SIYI *(glancing sideways):* Not right now it doesn't.
ZHANG: They said . . . *(embarrassed),* they said . . .
SIYI *(frowning):* They said what?
ZHANG: They said that the Old Master was extremely fussy about how the coffin was to be varnished and would not accept anything less than thirty coats. Now that they've put on the Fujian varnish and delivered the coffin *(smiles apologetically)* they would like some money from you. Money would . . .
SIYI *(laughing aloud slyly):* Why don't you ask them to get the money from the Old Master—tell them the coffin is not for me to sleep in. If they can't wait, tell them to take the coffin away. Having such a gloomy thing around depresses me.
ZHANG *(earnestly):* I think you should just let them have a little money, Da Nainai. This is Midautumn Festival and the coffin has already been varnished.

---

[13]A "qi pao" is a fitted Chinese dress with a Mandarin collar and snaps across one or both sides of the chest.

SIYI (*annoyed*): How much did the paint shop pay you to side with these rascals?

ZHANG: No, Da Nainai. You see . . .

Chen Naima,[14] *an old woman in her sixties, enters unsteadily through the living room door. She was a servant in the Zeng household for many years and was the wet-nurse for Da Nainai's husband. Forty years ago when the Zeng family was at its peak of glory, she entered the household as personal maid to the late Madam Zeng. She is a straightforward woman of peasant background who treats the Zeng children as her own. Recently her son has been urging her to return to her native village. She finally returned home for brief stays, but found that she missed the Zeng children very much. She has returned to visit them often, always bringing them small gifts from the countryside. This time she is returning with her grandson for the Midautumn Festival. Her steps are unsteady, and her hair frosted by streaks of white. Her face, however, shines with the glow of health. Her voice is loud and clear, attesting to the fact that she is still healthy and strong. She is a little deaf, and her face is often beaming with smiles. She is leading a comfortable life at home nowadays. A good-hearted chatterbox, she knows more about the Zeng family affairs than anyone else. While she always speaks her mind freely, no one in the Zeng household would dare to offend her. She is wearing a pale-blue blouse under a green woolen shawl, black pants, and black cloth shoes. A small red flower is planted in the gray bun on her head.*

ZHANG (*surprised*): Oh, Chen Nainai, you're here.

CHEN (*hurriedly, bowing to Siyi*): Da Nainai, really, the way these people come and collect money on the day of a festival! Is that the way merchants collect money?! (*Turns to Zhang; indignantly*): Zhang Shun, tell them to get the hell out of here! I've never seen anything like this, Da Nainai (*still panting with anger*).

SIYI (*smiling*): When did you arrive, Chen Naima?

[14]"Naima" literally means "wet-nurse."

ZHANG (apologizing): What's the matter, Chen Nainai?

CHEN (pointing at Zhang): Tell them to get the hell out of here! (Turning to Siyi and smiling with disdain): I have never seen anything like this, it really makes me mad! Can you believe they're blocking the doorway? (Turning to Zhang Shun; in anger): You go and tell them that this is a respectable household! If old Madam Zeng were still here we'd have these rascals locked up in no time! What's a few dollars to us? Even a poor old woman like me has had tens of thousands of dollars pass through my hands. They had the nerve to block the door and not let me come in.

SIYI (catching on; to flatter her, she says jokingly to Zhang): Heavens, who could have the audacity not to even recognize our Naima, Madam Chen?

CHEN (smiling happily): Da Nainai, that's not the point. I don't care whether they can tell who I am. What bothers me is that they don't know who this family is. When I first came here, only the powerful and wealthy were admitted. (To Zhang): Take your old grandfather, Zhang Cai, for example. With all the tips he collected from the guests in this household he bought himself land, got himself a wife, and had children and grandchildren. (Laughs and points at Zhang.) And then you came along, you little rascal.

ZHANG (encountering this seasoned colleague of his grandfather, all he can do is to agree and smile): Yes, yes, Chen Nainai.

SIYI: Have a seat, Chen Naima.

CHEN: Humph![15] Who are those slippery bastards anyhow? When I first came to this household, old Master Zeng was still the Young Master. (Indicates height with her hand.) And Young Master was only this big. Then it was . . .

SIYI (helping her to sit down; consoling): Sit down and don't get so upset. What happened, Chen Naima?

CHEN: Humph! Once Midautumn Festival is over . . .

---

[15]An interjection of annoyance or anger.

SIYI: Chen Naima, how did they treat you?

CHEN *(hard of hearing)*: What?

ZHANG: She's hard of hearing, she can't hear you. Da Nainai, don't pay any attention to her. She'll never stop.

CHEN: What was that?

ZHANG *(loudly)*: Da Nainai wants to know if those collectors pushed you around.

CHEN *(understands and immediately takes several bills out of her pocket)*: Look! They blocked the doorway and shoved these into my hands, and insisted that I bring them in to you.

SIYI *(takes the bills from her)*: Oh, this!

CHEN *(hitting the back of her hand against her palm)*: See what I mean? Those good-for-nothings!

SIYI *(going through the bills)*: Humph. Even the mounters are sending us bills. Zhang Shun, tell the messenger from Da Shu Zhai[16] that the master isn't home.

CHEN: Oh, how is Master Wenqing?

SIYI *(takes out some money)*: Give them twenty dollars and tell them to deduct it from the down payment. We'll have to wait for the master to come back to find out whether he likes the mounting job. Then we can settle our accounts with them.

ZHANG: But how about the tailor, the fruit market, and then there's the one who varnished the coffin . . .

SIYI *(impatiently)*: That can wait, that can wait. We'll talk to the Old Master later.

ZHANG *(pointing to the door on the left; in a low voice)*: Gu Laoye[17] has been complaining all morning that the garden wall by his room is starting to collapse. He wants to know whether it will be fixed.

SIYI *(displeased)*: Tell him that it's not a matter of whether we

---

[16]Name of the scroll mounting shop.

[17]A respectful term for the son-in-law of the head of the family; in this case, Jiang Tai.

want to fix it, but whether we have the money to do it. Tell
him to be patient because the master has plans to sell the
house.

ZHANG *(unwittingly)*: Da Nainai, the servants' quarters are also
leaking, on rainy nights, like last night . . .

SIYI *(coldly)*: I'm sorry, but I don't have the money. I'll talk to the
Old Master and have him build a mansion especially for
you.

*(Zhang does not know how to reply. Voices calling his name can be
heard from outside: "Mr. Zhang, Mr. Zhang.")*

ZHANG: Coming! *(Exits through living room door.)*

SIYI *(turning to Chen Naima, says warmly)*: Naima, you must be
tired after your trip. Are you all right?

CHEN *(disappointed, but unwilling to accept not seeing her Master
Wenqing)*: What a pity, Da Nainai, that my Young Master is
not home . . .

SIYI: Don't worry, your Young Master *(pointing to the door on the
right side)* is still sleeping. He'll be out shortly to pay his
respects to his Naima.

CHEN *(laughing)*: Da Nainai, please don't poke fun at me. Even
though I'm his Naima, a servant is a servant and a master
is a master. Since when does a master approaching forty,
with a son and daughter-in-law, come to pay me . . .

SIYI *(faking respect)*: In that case, Naima, let me bow to you first.

CHEN *(on her feet immediately, helping Siyi up)*: Enough, enough.
God forbid! You, Da Nainai, are already a mother-in-law!
Ai! . . .

*(The two continue this game briefly; Siyi, naturally, does not really
want to bow to this servant. Then . . .)*

SIYI *(ending with a giggle)*: Ai! But I must!

CHEN *(delighted)*: Yes! I was startled by what you just said! I was
thinking the reason I walked all the way to town was . . .

SIYI *(interrupting)*: To see your Master Wenqing.

CHEN *(her intentions exposed, startled, she giggles nervously)*: Oh
you, you're so clever. *(Clears her throat.)* I'm also here to see

you, Da Nainai, Miss Su, the Old Master, Madam Cai, the Young Master Ting and his wife. Imagine. Visiting a family this size and leaving without seeing them all . . .

SIYI: But why must you leave so soon?

CHEN: I told my son and daughter-in-law that I'd be back this evening . . .

SIYI: How can that be? You can't come all the way to Peking from the village without staying awhile.

CHEN *(still proud but touched):* Ha, I've already spent forty years of my life here! I didn't even go home when my son got married. Tell me, which family is really mine? Da Nainai, my grandson brought along some little presents from the country for you.

SIYI: Really, Naima, you shouldn't have!

CHEN *(sincerely):* Oh, it's only a few little things. *(Walks toward the living room, smiling.)* If I weren't such a shameless fool, I wouldn't be . . . *(searching in vain).* Xiao Zhuer! Xiao Zhuer! That boy can disappear in no time. Xiao Zhuer! Xiao Zhuer! *(Calling, she leaves the living room and walks into the courtyard in search of her grandson.)*

(The flute-like sounds of the pigeons' bamboo whistles can be heard overhead, soothing and relaxing. Beyond the wall, a cold-drink peddler is knocking on a "bing jiang"—a shiny brass instrument in the form of two cups which, when knocked together, make a clear ringing noise. Full and resonant, the beat is, "DING cha, DING cha, DING DING cha, cha cha DING DING cha." The peddler has a clear Peking accent and yells as if he were very happy: "Cool as ice! Sweet and nice! Rosy flavor try it twice!"[18] At this point the peddler raises his voice and sings with the beat. "Sour plum soup, special flavor! Sour plum soup!" The bing jiang rings continuously: "DING cha cha, DING cha cha, cha cha DING DING cha." Zeng Siyi walks quietly over to the suitcase and slowly arranges the clothes inside.)

---

[18]Literally, "Thirst-quenching and cool with rose-flavor and sugar! If you don't believe it, taste it and see!"

SIYI (*suddenly turns her head to the right*): Wenqing, are you up yet?

(*No response*).

SIYI: Wenqing, your Naima is here.

VOICE OF ZENG WENQING (*from the room on the right; hollow and weary*): I know. Why don't you invite her in?

SIYI: Invite her in? Reeking of garlic! The whole room smells of it when she's here. Maybe you can take it, but I can't. Are you really leaving today or not? Your suitcase is all packed.

VOICE OF WENQING (*from inside, slowly and leisurely*): Are the pigeons flying?

SIYI (*paying no attention to him*): Are you leaving or not?

VOICE OF WENQING (*from inside, contemplative*): The pigeons are really flying high today! I can hardly hear their whistles.

SIYI (*walks toward door on right*): Listen, what do you really plan to do? What do you really . . .

VOICE OF WENQING (*from inside, drawing out his voice, troubled*): I'm leaving, I'm leaving. I really have to leave.

SIYI (*walks to bedroom door, raises curtain, pushes open the door, and lets out a small cry as if she has seen something ominous*): Oh, how could you?

At this point Chen Naima's voice and footsteps can be heard in the living room. Siyi turns her head and listens attentively. The two bedroom doors are closed immediately from the inside.

Naima walks in with Xiao Zhuer, her grandson. Xiao Zhuer is fourteen or fifteen. His head is shaved, and he is wearing new clothes which peasant children only wear at New Year's and during other important festivals—cotton socks, cloth shoes; his pants are tied at the ankle with strings. He is wearing a coarse, blue cotton "chang shan"[19] with short sleeves and a loose collar. The "chang shan" is too small for him and does not even reach his knees; the color has faded from overwashing and is mended behind the collar with red cloth. It has shrunk and fits him very tightly, showing his plump physique. He is holding a

---

[19] A Chinese gown worn by men.

clay toy in one hand, a "gua da zui" in the form of a rabbit or pig—a movable toy animated by a string running through the center. In his other hand is a bamboo pigeon cage and under his arm a live hen. The servant, Zhang Shun, follows with a big bamboo basket containing chickens, eggs, and vegetables. The two of them stand on the side dripping with perspiration.

CHEN: Get in here, get in here! *(Grumbling.)* Look at you, sweating like that. Who said you could drink sour plum soup? Here it's autumn already and you're still drinking cold things. You'll get an upset stomach for sure. *(Turns to Zhang):* Zhang Shun, you were with him. How could you let him get away with this? *(Points at the toy.)* Who bought this "gua da zui" for you?

XIAO: *(looking sideways at Zhang Shun):* He did. Mr. Zhang.

CHEN *(turning to Zhang Shun, half smiling, half scolding):* What are you smiling about? You can't win me over by buying things for him.

SIYI: Let him go.

CHEN: Xiao Zhuer, you haven't kowtowed to Da Nainai yet. Put those things down first, put them down.

(Xiao Zhuer puts the pigeon cage down and throws the hen into the basket that Zhang is holding.)

SIYI: There's no need for that. He must be tired from the long trip.

CHEN *(seeing that Xiao Zhuer has not put the toy down, grabs it from him):* Put the "gua da zui" down, no one is going to steal it from you. *(Hands the toy to Zhang Shun.)*

(Zhang Shun is helpless, already overloaded with the things he is carrying.)

SIYI: No, no, it's too much trouble.

CHEN *(laughing):* Look at this little bumpkin. I've been telling him what to do all the way here, and once he gets to town he forgets everything. *(She walks up to Xiao Zhuer and tries to push him down.)* Kowtow, my little one!

(*Xiao Zhuer looks dumbfoundedly at his grandmother, not knowing what to do. When Chen Naima lets go of him, he suddenly goes down on the floor, nods his head once on the floor and gets up immediately.*)

SIYI (*has a red money envelope ready in her hand*): Xiao Zhuer, you clumsy little thing, I wish you a long and happy life. Come, take this and buy yourself some snacks.

(*Xiao Zhuer stands there dumbly.*)

CHEN (*to Siyi*): Honestly! Once again I've caused you to spend money! (*To her grandson*): Go ahead, you can take it. It's a gift from your grandmother's friends. (*Xiao Zhuer walks up and takes it.*) Say thank you! (*Xiao Zhuer takes the toy back from the servant and looks down with a stupid grin on his face.*) This child can't do anything right. He can't stand up right, he can't sit right, and he can't even kowtow right. Da Nainai, please sit down. Ai, it's such a long trip in this hot weather. (*Pulls out a stool and sits down.*) And the whole way I had this child to take care of . . .

ZHANG (*growing impatient*): Chen Nainai, I'm still holding all this!

CHEN (*turns and smiles*): Oh, see how forgetful I am! Da Nainai (*brings Siyi over to the basket and rummages through as she talks*) there's really nothing fancy to bring you from the country. I've just picked some leeks, celery, kohlrabi, cucumbers, green peppers, cowpeas, these few things . . .

SIYI: Oh, you shouldn't have brought so much.

CHEN: Oh, and there's a little millet, some eggs, and a couple of old hens.

SIYI: It looks like you're moving your whole house here. Honestly! And to carry these things such a long way, we really can't . . . (*Turns to Zhang*): Zhang Shun, take them inside.

CHEN (*to Zhang*): And there're two big turnips here somewhere. (*Rummages.*)

ZHANG (*laughing*): Don't bother looking. I ate them already. (*Hurriedly carries the basket out through the living room door.*)

XIAO (*secretively*): Grandmother.

CHEN: What's the matter?

XIAO (*in a low voice*): Should I take it out or not?

CHEN (*puzzled*): What?

(*Xiao Zhuer gives his grandmother a sudden sharp glance and lifts the pigeon cage.*)

CHEN (*suddenly remembering*): Oh! (*Very anxiously*): Where is it? Where is it?

XIAO (*looking very apologetic, pulls a tiny gray pigeon out from under his shirt; its head feathers are ruffled, its wings are a glossy color, and it has several purple spots on its little body; it is obviously a rare species*): Here it is!

CHEN (*picks up the pigeon; her voice trembling with joy, she says to it*): Good boy, my dear, so here you are! No wonder I felt there was something missing. (*To Da Nainai*): Look at this little fellow! They were a pair and I got them especially for Master Wenqing. On the way here, he [*meaning the grandson*] couldn't stop playing with them and one flew away just like that. Master Wenqing is very fortunate. The better-looking one didn't get away. Da Nainai, just feel those feathers. (*Forces the bird into her hands.*) Feel that little heart beating.

SIYI (*does not like little creatures such as pigeons; moves away, but manages to force a smile*): All right, all right, all right. (*Calls to the door to the right*): Wenqing, your Chen Naima has brought you a pigeon again!

CHEN (*cannot restrain herself from calling*): Master Wenqing.

VOICE OF WENQING (*from inside*): Chen Naima.

CHEN (*with pigeon in hand, wants to present this "valuable gift" to the Young Master immediately*): I'm going to show it to him. (*Walking toward his bedroom as she speaks.*)

SIYI (*hurriedly*): Don't go in yet.

CHEN (*a little startled*): Why?

SIYI: He, he's not up yet.

CHEN (*still very happy*): That doesn't matter. I can talk to Master Wenqing by his bedside. (*Moves toward the door again.*)

SIYI: No, don't go in. The room is a mess.

CHEN (*kindly*): Oh, it doesn't matter. (*Moves toward the door again.*)

SIYI *(calling out)*: Wenqing, are you dressed?

VOICE OF WENQING *(from inside)*: I'm getting dressed now.

CHEN *(laughing wholeheartedly)*: At my age, there's nothing to be shy about. *(Approaching the door and pushing it.)*

VOICE OF WENQING *(from inside, loudly)*: Don't come in. Don't come in!

SIYI *(blocking her way)*: Just wait a moment. He doesn't like people watching him getting dressed.

CHEN *(a little disappointed)*: Oh well, never mind. You can't change people's ways. *(Kindly)*: Da Nainai, I was still dressing him when he was sixteen years old. *(Hands the pigeon to Xiao Zhuer.)* Put this back. *(Unable to refrain from calling to the door)*: Master Wenqing, how have you been?

SIYI *(pulls out a stool at the same time)*: Have a seat while you talk to him.

VOICE OF WENQING *(from inside, warmly)*: Fine, and how about you?

CHEN *(loudly)*: Oh, fine! *(Her face shines with happiness.)* I have a new granddaughter.

(Xiao Zhuer quietly places the pigeon back in its cage.)

VOICE OF WENQING *(from inside)*: Congratulations.

CHEN *(loudly)*: Yes, and she's a fat one too! *(Sits down.)*

SIYI: He said "congratulations."

CHEN: Huh, congratulations for what? It's a girl.

VOICE OF WENQING *(from inside)*: You should stay for a few days.

CHEN *(craning her neck; loudly)*: Yes, and she's almost a month old.

SIYI: He asked you to stay longer.

CHEN *(shaking her head)*: No, I have to go soon.

VOICE OF WENQING *(didn't hear what she said)*: Eh?

CHEN *(stands up; loudly)*: I have to leave soon, Young Master.

VOICE OF WENQING: Why so soon?

CHEN: Eh?

VOICE OF WENQING *(loudly)*: Why so soon?

CHEN *(still not hearing well)*: What?

XIAO *(cannot resist laughing):* Grandmother, you're really deaf. He asked you why you're in such a hurry to leave.

CHEN *(her voice strained from shouting, she unconsciously repeats what he said):* In such a hurry to leave? *(Slightly annoyed, but manages to laugh.)* What an awkward way to carry on a conversation. Enough of this, I'll wait for him to come out. Da Nainai, I'll go into the courtyard and see Miss Su first.

SIYI: Fine. I'll have someone fetch you later. *(Takes a string of red candies from a plate on the table.)* Xiao Zhuer, these candies are for you *(handing them to him).*

CHEN: Say thank you. *(Xiao Zhuer grins stupidly, takes the candies, and starts eating them immediately.)* Always eating, always eating! *(She tries to take the candy out of his mouth.)* Stop eating that! Look at you! *(Xiao Zhuer keeps staring greedily at the red candies in her hand.)* And put that "gua da zui" down and come with me!

(Xiao Zhuer puts the toy down reluctantly. Naima takes him by the hand and exits through the small door of the study.)

SIYI: How obnoxious! *(Sets the colorful toy aside and picks up the pigeon cage.)*

VOICE OF WENQING *(from inside):* Chen Naima!

SIYI: She's gone.

Zeng Wenqing, Siyi's husband, strolls in through the bedroom door on the right. He is tall and thin and is wearing a long, loose gown of a subdued but elegant color. There is a certain indolence in his appearance and mannerisms. His coloring is pale; he has a wide forehead and high cheekbones. His bloodless lips appear extremely sensitive. A look of despair clouds his sunken eyes, sad and lifeless. He is often lost in reverie, and the veins on his forehead protrude slightly.

He was born and raised in a family of scholars in Peking. Chess, poetry, and painting naturally occupy most of his time. Life in Peking is leisurely—kite flying in the spring, yachting on the North Sea[20] on summer evenings, admiring the foliage at the Western Mountain in the

---

[20]A famous tourist spot in Peking.

autumn, and painting by the window on snowy winter mornings. When lonely he writes poetry; when relaxed he indulges in tea drinking. Half his life has been spent in this hollow and leisurely existence.

He was spoiled from childhood by his mother. Although not in good health, he married early. He is a clever person in small matters, but appears lazy and lethargic. He seems too lazy to move, to think, to talk, to walk, to rise, to meet people, or to attend to any serious matter that demands his energy. His pessimistic attitude toward life has depressed him to the extent that he is unable to express the torment in his heart. He is too lazy to feel his own emotions, so lazy that one sees that "his life is an empty shell."

He is still buttoning his lined silk shirt as he enters.

WENQING *(smile fading on his face):* Is she gone? Why didn't you ask her to stay a little longer?

SIYI *(ignoring his question):* Here's the pigeon she brought you *(handing it over to Wenqing).*

WENQING *(lifts up the pigeon cage):* Poor old woman; and she had to walk all that distance. *(Admires the pigeon.)* Look, this is a "phoenix head"! "Short beak!" *(Happily):* There should be a pair, how come . . . *(lifts his head and sees an angry face staring at him).*

SIYI: Wenqing, why did you have to start smoking that again?

(With a very sad expression on his face, Wenqing sets the pigeon cage down.)

SIYI *(grumpily):* Only yesterday, the old man was asking about you. He wanted to know whether you'd thrown away your opium pipes. I told him you had. *(Shouting):* I just can't believe it! The bitterness we've suffered. And then you stopped smoking altogether. Now you want to cause trouble just when you're about to leave?

WENQING *(sighs as he sits down):* Ai, don't bother me. Just let me smoke in peace.

SIYI *(disdainfully):* Who cares? But we do have to be a little careful about maintaining some respect around here. Are you really going to live up to what your brother-in-law said about you? He said that you wouldn't dare leave this place, that you'll never be able to do anything, and that you'll waste your life away smoking opium, drinking tea, playing with pigeons, painting, and all that!

WENQING (*unaffected*): Who cares what he says? Aren't I leaving soon?

SIYI: If you're leaving, then don't embarrass me. Stop this perverse behavior.

WENQING (*miserably*): Don't I do everything you tell me to do? What more do you want? (*Stares ahead aimlessly.*)

SIYI (*needling him, coldly*): Don't look so pathetic. I'm not a witch. And don't act as if I've been unfair to you all this time. I don't want the reputation of an indomitable wife. I can't live up to it. (*Walks to the suitcase.*)

WENQING (*stares at the pigeon cage expressionlessly*): Forget it. I'll be gone by tonight.

SIYI (*opens the suitcase; turns to Wenqing*): Listen here. I'm not forcing you to go out and find a job. So don't let anyone think that that's my idea. If you run into any trouble out there, all your relatives will blame it on me, saying that you're there suffering while I stay home having a fine time; it's Da Nainai's fault again. (*Grumbles as she goes through the contents of the suitcase.*) Let me tell you, I've had enough of this household. Humph! When your mother was alive, she treated me miserably. Now that she's gone, I get the same abuse from my daughter-in-law. The old people, the young people, and then there's you in the middle.

WENQING (*getting tired of her grumbling, searches for a new topic*): Oh, this bamboo ink painting is already hung.

SIYI (*looking sideways*): There it is, all right . . .

WENQING (*walks up to the painting*): The mounting isn't bad.

SIYI (*sarcastically*): I think the painting is even better. Really, extraordinarily fine! One can paint, and the other can write. The scholar and the beauty—what a natural pair!

WENQING *(feels stifled)*: Don't make something out of nothing. You're making fun of Miss Su again.

SIYI *(disdainfully)*: Strange. Why are you being so defensive? What did I say about you two? What's so remarkable about Miss Su's painting that you decided to inscribe it with your own poem, and even take it personally to be mounted? Let me tell you, I'm not narrow-minded. If my husband wants a concubine, I'm all for it. *(Boastfully)*: If I were a man, I'd have seven or eight concubines. Men! They're all alike! What do they care about besides wine and sex and money? *(Caustically)*: But a woman like Miss Su . . .

WENQING *(a bit annoyed)*: Don't talk like that. She's still an unmarried lady!

SIYI: That's strange. *(Says penetratingly, with a strange laugh)*: What's she to you that you have to protect her like that?

WENQING *(sincerely)*: A person who has no mother and father, living in our household; you mean to tell me you have no sympathy for her?

SIYI *(grinning cunningly)*: You give her your sympathy; do you think she has any for you? *(Pointing at him)*: Don't think she's a quiet, kind, and unassuming lady. *(Proudly)*: I know what kind of a woman she really is! *(Grumbling)*: Women like that are all so conniving. The less they say, the more they're scheming. You think she's still single because she likes being with your Old Master? You think such a pretty and talented woman chooses to remain an old maid just so that she can take care of the old man, and suffer? *(Laughs coldly.)* I'm not making any wild accusations. You think about it for yourself.

WENQING *(stares at her coldly)*: I can't think of anything.

SIYI *(exploding)*: If you can't figure that out then you're a fool!

WENQING *(loneliness and sadness comes across his face; he sighs)*: Ai, let's drop this clever guessing game of yours! *(He lowers his head, strolls toward the study, and stops at the desk, trying to find something.)*

SIYI *(feels wronged)*: Me clever? Humph. No clever person would suffer in your house for twenty years. I should have learned from those modern wives a long time ago. I should have spent my time in restaurants and movie houses, and handed this household over to my daughter-in-law so that she could take care of it. That would have saved me a lot of trouble. At least the old man wouldn't sulk at me all day as if I owed him the world. *(Self-pitying)*: Ai, I have the temperament of an aristocrat but the fate of a maid! I'm almost forty, and yet I still worry about answering to my father-in-law and daughter-in-law, and to you too. *(Picks up a cup of ginseng soup.)* Enough of that. Here, drink this ginseng soup before it gets cold.

WENQING *(frowns, but tolerates the conversation; rummaging, he suddenly pulls a scroll of unmounted painting out of the drawer of the desk; furiously)*: Look, look, who did this? *(A big hole about the size of a palm can be seen in the mid-section of the painting. It looks as if an animal has been chewing on it.)*

SIYI *(sets the cup down)*: What?

WENQING *(shaking the painting)*: Look, look at it!

SIYI *(enjoying the misfortune of her husband; lightly)*: Don't tell me that your brother-in-law did this.

WENQING *(returns to the desk, searching through the drawers)*: Rats! It must be the rats! *(Walks up to Siyi, waving the painting in the air.)* Haven't I told you that this old house is infested with rats? I asked you to get some rat poison but you didn't do it.

SIYI: I already did, my master *(sarcastically)*. But they're just as bad as before, only a bit more cunning. They won't touch the poison; instead, they nibble on your favorite things.

WENQING *(disappointed and hurt)*: This painting is ruined.

SIYI *(coldheartedly)*: What does it matter? Can't you just go and ask Miss Su to paint you another one?

WENQING *(growing more and more impatient; loudly)*: You . . . *(Suddenly realizes the futility of reasoning with her and feels a numbing sense of disappointment creeping over him; sitting very still with his head lowered, he stares at the damaged painting in silence.)* I painted this myself.

SIYI *(slightly surprised, but maintaining a cool tone of voice):* That's strange. Why does it bother you so much that a few little rats chew up your painting? Yet you act as if nothing had happened when a pack of big rats has been eating up this house, our property, year round.

WENQING *(sighs, throws the painting on the floor, stands, and smiles sadly):* Ai, we should share whatever we have.

SIYI *(angrily):* Share whatever we have? What did your ancestors hand down to you that's worth bragging about? While the old man is alive you can claim half of it. But when he dies . . .

(Suddenly, a voice is heard cursing and scolding from stage left. The tone is condescending and arrogant; the voice rambles on and on, as if accustomed to ordering and scolding servants.)

VOICE FROM STAGE LEFT: Get out, get out, get out. Lousy bastards, sons of bitches!

SIYI *(to Wenqing):* Listen!

VOICE FROM STAGE LEFT *(as if a window has been opened, the voice is now screaming into the courtyard):* Zhang Shun! Zhang Shun! Lin Ma! Lin Ma!

WENQING *(walks to the doorway of the living room as if to help the voice in calling):* Zhang Shun, Zhang . . .

SIYI *(pouting, with bulging eyes, as if to pick a fight):* What are you shouting about?

(Wenqing falls silent.)

SIYI *(in a low voice):* Let him yell. If he's not beating the chickens, he's cursing the dogs. *(Laughs angrily.)* Humph, this must be his going-away gift to you.

VOICE FROM STAGE LEFT *(shouting):* Zhang Shun! It's only Mid-autumn Festival. Have you all dropped dead or what!

SIYI *(laughing maliciously):* Listen to him!

VOICE FROM STAGE LEFT *(drawn out):* Zhang—Shun!

WENQING *(tries to help again, walking forward):* Zhang . . .

SIYI *(blocking his way; firmly):* Don't help him. I want to see what kind of tantrum our Gu Laoye is going to throw this time!

(Noise of shattering glasses and plates, followed by the sound of a woman sobbing. A short pause.)

WENQING *(in a low voice):* Sister just got over her illness, and here she's crying again.

SIYI *(laughing coldly and disdainfully):* That good-for-nothing. He has nothing better to do than bully his wife all day long. And to think that he has even studied abroad. What nonsense!

VOICE FROM STAGE LEFT *(right after Siyi's line):* Lousy bastards!

(A bang, and then more shattering noises.)

VOICE FROM STAGE LEFT *(barking):* Has everyone dropped dead?

SIYI *(getting angrier and angrier, takes a stride forward):* This time he's really going too far! These things belong to our family, we had to pay good money for them!

WENQING *(blocks her way; in low voice):* Siyi, don't start with him.

(Zhang Shun enters hurriedly through the door that leads to the living room.)

ZHANG *(hurriedly):* Did Gu Laoye call me?

WENQING: Hurry up and get in there.

(Zhang Shun runs into the left room.)

SIYI *(furious):* "We should share whatever we have." *(To Wenqing):* Do you think a person like him appreciates your generosity? Who does he think he is? He's nothing but a crook. He embezzled money, and the law's still after him. He's hiding here in his father-in-law's house. He might as well give up that arrogant air of his. *(Points to the door.)* And I suppose he's celebrating the holidays by smashing things. I just don't understand why . . .

Zeng Ting, son of Siyi and Wenqing, enters excitedly through the living room door. He is dripping with perspiration.

Zeng Ting is only seventeen years old, but he has been married for two years. His wife is a year older. When they were still in the care of wet-nurses, the grandfathers on both sides decided that the two families were well matched and arranged for the marriage. Since the grandparents were eagerly looking forward to having great-grandchildren, the couple got married two years before Zeng Ting entered high school. It was a time when other children were enjoying basketball games, romping in snow, or even fighting. Instead, an auspicious day was selected for their wedding. In the midst of deafening firecrackers, cymbals, and drums, this young couple—he fifteen and she sixteen—frightened and confused, were led like a pair of lambs to unite in matrimony before the glow of the dragon and phoenix candles. They bowed once, twice, and a third time. From then on they were left to share a cold bridal chamber for two years and seven months. No great-grandson was born, while the grandmother passed away during the first month of their marriage. Zeng Ting and his wife are like strangers. They hardly talk to each other but suffer together like a pair of ill-treated animals. When he returns from the study every night, he must go to his grandfather's quarters and recite from such texts as Zhao Ming's Anthology of Literature *and* Longwen Bianyin.[21] *Occasionally, he also has to practice his calligraphy or compose monotonous couplets. He usually returns to his room after the second watch, exhausted. Seeing his wife still sitting silently under the dim light, he gets into bed and sinks into deep sleep without a word.*

After seven months in school he has begun to show signs of change. Under the influence of his vivacious peers, he regained some of his youthful vitality. It was only then that members of the family began to discover that this quiet little adult still possessed some childlike qualities. The sudden change in his behavior has caused his elders displeasure. Even distant relatives were surprised, as if they felt that all the children of the Zeng family should be mature, proper, and scholarly. He is in-

[21]*Zhao Ming's Anthology* is a literary collection of poems, prose, and other major works compiled during the Liang dynasty (502–557). *Longwen Bianyin* is a popular book of recitations for children consisting of different stories in rhyming verse. It was believed that memorization of its contents could enhance the learning ability of the child.

*creasingly tempted by life outdoors, as he starts to appreciate the breeze
and the warmth of the sun. He likes watching little animals at play,
and people climbing trees to pick dates. He loves to fly his kite alone by
the bank of the river. Especially of late, he has been invited to participate
in all kinds of child's play by the daughter of an anthropologist who has
recently moved into the household. For reasons unknown to himself, he
has been following this vivacious, candid girl around like someone following a torch in the dark of evening. She in turn enjoys his compan-
ionship, and constantly asks him interesting questions that he finds
difficult to answer. Zeng Ting has begun to feel that a new world is
unfolding before him. His heart suddenly races under the impulse of a
boy in love for the first time. Actually, it is the first time he has expe-
rienced anything like this. He gradually forgets his usual proper manners. At times, at her instigation, he jumps and runs with her; and at
her insistence, wrestles with her in his shy, hesitant way. He has simply
forgotten that he is seventeen, and, as his mother and grandfather have
frequently reminded him, an adult with family responsibilities.*

*He is handsome in a fragile way, like his father. His face is pale
and thin. His dark, sunken eyes are like still, ageless ponds. He is
wearing a long, lined gown of subdued color, cloth shoes, and white
cotton pants. Perspiration can be seen on his forehead.*

TING (*suddenly sees his mother and stops*): Mother!

WENQING: Back from school?

TING: Yes, Father.

SIYI (*continues her grumbling*): Remember, Ting, don't ever be like
    your uncle no matter how poor you are. Even if you have
    to starve, don't live off your father-in-law. Look at Uncle
    Yuan who's staying with us. He pays his rent at the begin-
    ning of each month, and pays for whatever he eats. People
    respect him even if he is a little odd. I've never seen anyone
    like our Gu Laoye, just like a stone in an outhouse, both
    foul and hard.

VOICE OF A GIRL (*from the courtyard*): Zeng Ting! Zeng Ting!

WENQING: Listen. Who's calling you?

VOICE OF GIRL *(from courtyard):* Zeng Ting! Zeng Ting!

TING *(cannot help but answer, even in the presence of his mother):* Yes! . . .

VOICE OF GIRL *(from courtyard; yells laughingly):* Come on out, Zeng Ting, I've taken my clothes off already!

SIYI *(severely):* Who's that?

TING: Uncle Yuan's daughter.

SIYI: What does she want you for?

TING *(timidly):* She, she wants to have a water fight.

SIYI *(astonished):* What? A grown girl having a water fight without her clothes on!

TING *(trying to explain):* She, she's always like that.

SIYI *(scolding sarcastically):* And you still play with her?

TING *(awkwardly):* She, she wants to.

SIYI *(sternly):* Don't you go out there! Water-fighting on Mid-autumn Festival, have you lost your mind? This is what I don't like about the Yuan family, absolutely no discipline. He's really spoiled that daughter of his!

VOICE OF GIRL *(from courtyard; raising her voice):* Zeng—Ting!

TING *(wants to answer but dares not):* Ai!

SIYI *(interrupts immediately):* Don't you answer her!

TING *(wants to tell the girl what is going on):* Then let me . . . *(He takes a step.)*

SIYI *(stops him):* Don't you dare! *(To Zeng Ting):* You think you're still a child? You're seventeen and you're married. Your grandfather was already supporting a family when he was your age! *(Suddenly):* Is your wife home yet?

TING *(listens to her painfully and replies in a low voice):* We already telephoned her.

SIYI: What'd she say?

TING *(timidly):* I didn't call. I asked Auntie Su to.

SIYI *(angrily):* Why didn't you call her yourself? I told you to. Why didn't you?

VOICE OF GIRL *(from courtyard, almost simultaneously):* Zeng Ting, where're you hiding?

TING (*perturbed, not knowing whom to answer*): Auntie Su wanted to ask her to buy some sandalwood.

VOICE OF GIRL (*from courtyard, impatiently*): If you don't answer me, I'm going to be angry.

SIYI (*seeing that Zeng Ting is being tempted again, she blurts out angrily before he even moves*): Don't you move! If Auntie Su wants sandalwood, ask her to go buy it herself. (*Stubbornly*): I asked you to call Ruizhen and you wouldn't listen to me. Why don't you ever listen to me?

(*Zeng Ting glances at her and lowers his head without replying.*)

WENQING (*sighing*): The two of them have nothing to say to each other, so let it be. Why force it? Forcing them doesn't do any good.

VOICE OF GIRL (*from courtyard, loudly*): Zeng—Ting!

SIYI (*facing direction of voice*): How obnoxious! (*Turns to Wenqing*): Forcing them doesn't do any good! You're going to spoil them rotten. Let me ask you this. Who told her she could go home to her parents on Midautumn Festival? What kind of manners does she have? She knows we're having problems here now and that we're short of servants. Even I have to help Zhang Shun in the kitchen. (*Cold-heartedly*): Humph! She's not even from a wealthy family and she's developed this little princess attitude. (*To Zeng Ting, angrily*): Tell her that she's to keep us better informed of her whereabouts. She's married into an old family of scholars here; and though we might not have any rules or regulations, we are particular about manners.

A big and healthy Miss Yuan Yuan—the beloved daughter of a scholar who has devoted his life to anthropology—enters running through the parlor door. She has a bucket of cold water in her hand and is wearing a short-sleeved shirt, sneakers, and [Western] boys' shorts that leave her round and healthy legs exposed. Standing by the door, she looks spiritedly around the room, her face full of mischief. She tumbles around in the house all day long, without pausing for a moment. While she frequently engages in games with boys, everything about her is natural and simple, straightforward and candid. Her hair is cut short. Perspiration is running down her red, flushed face.

YUAN *(pointing to Zeng Ting):* Zeng Ting, here you are! I've been looking high and low for you. *(Gaily runs up with a bucket of water as she speaks, embarrassing Zeng Ting. He is absolutely helpless in the presence of his mother.)*

TING *(screaming):* Water! Water! *(Hides behind his father.)*

SIYI *(surprised and a little frightened):* Don't splash that cold water around here! *(Restrains Yuan Yuan.)* Let me ask you a question, Miss Yuan.

YUAN *(turns with a big smile on her face):* What's that?

SIYI *(searching for a question):* Where is your father?

YUAN *(sets down the bucket and pretends to be serious):* He's in his room making a drawing of the "Peking Man." *(Screams suddenly and catches Zeng Ting like a cat pouncing on a mouse).* So you're running away, huh? Let's just see how far you can get!

TING *(laughs embarrassedly):* You! You let me go!

YUAN *(excitedly):* Come on, let's go out and settle this outside.

SIYI *(displeased):* Miss Yuan!

YUAN: Let's go.

WENQING *(smiling):* Yuan Yuan, do you want a little gift?

YUAN *(suddenly remembers; lets go of Zeng Ting):* Oh yes, Uncle Zeng, you promised me a big kite. You told me you had one. Won't you find it for me?

WENQING *(laughingly):* Autumn is not the season for flying kites.

YUAN *(stubbornly):* But you promised! I want to fly it, I want to!

WENQING *(smiling):* I found you a "centipede" kite.

YUAN *(leaps for joy):* Where is it! *(Holds out her hand.)* Let me have it!

WENQING *(cannot help but smile):* The centipede has been eaten by rats.

YUAN *(suspicious):* You're kidding me.

WENQING: What could I do? The rats were hungry and ate the glue off the kite.

YUAN (*stamps her foot*): But you said! (*About to cry*).

WENQING (*trying to comfort her*): Don't cry, don't cry. I still have another one.

YUAN (*smiling behind tears*): Really? I don't believe you.

WENQING: Ting, bring that goldfish kite in here from the study (*pointing in the direction of the study*).

TING (*almost leaping for joy*): I'll get it.

SIYI (*stops him with a bark*): Ting, what do you think you're doing? (*Zeng Ting suppresses his joy and walks to the study like a grown man.*)

YUAN (*follows him hurriedly*): Zeng Ting! (*Takes his hand.*) Hurry up! (*Drags him over to the study and sees a colorful kite covered with dust. Overjoyed, she lets out a little cry.*) Oh, it's so big! (*immediately snatching it*).

TING (*an unusually joyful smile crosses his face; trembling*): Let go, let me do it. (*Holds up the kite.*)

YUAN (*struggling with him*): Let go. Let me!

TING: You're so clumsy you're going to rip it.

YUAN (*screaming*): Let me! Let me! Let me do it! Your father made it for me!

(*The two struggle for the goldfish.*)

SIYI (*simultaneously*): Ting!

TING (*gasping for breath, yells out*): No, no. (*Looking at Yuan Yuan, fights over the kite with her, excited and happy. He grabs the kite with his pale and almost translucent fingers, nearly losing the kite to the strong arms of Yuan Yuan.*)

YUAN (*yelling simultaneously*): Let me, let me!

(*Zeng Ting suddenly lets out a cry, sets down the kite, and stares at his bleeding finger.*)

YUAN (*a little frightened*): What's the matter?

SIYI (*blamingly*): See what happens? (*Walks up to Zeng Ting, reprimanding.*) Look, you're bleeding.

WENQING (*looking at Zeng Ting*): Did you cut yourself?

TING *(holding his finger):* Yes.

YUAN *(concerned):* Does it hurt?

TING *(embarrassed):* A little.

SIYI *(taking hold of Zeng Ting):* Hurry and put some medicine on it.

YUAN *(confidently):* Oh, you don't need to do that. *(She bends her head and sucks on his injured finger.)*

TING *(taken aback by this):* Oh! *(Flushed with excitement and gratitude, he shyly breaks his mother's grip.)* Never mind, mother, it's all right.

YUAN *(spits and lets go of his hand happily):* There—does it still hurt?

TING *(softly):* No, not anymore. *(Yuan Yuan picks up the bucket of water suddenly.)*

TING AND SIYI *(excitedly):* Oh no!

YUAN *(smiles at Zeng Ting):* I'll let you go this time. I won't throw this bucket of water on you. *(Prods Zeng Ting.)* Let's go fly the kite. *(Zeng Ting immediately picks up the kite.)* 'Bye Auntie Zeng. *(Yuan Yuan skips out, pushing Zeng Ting along with her. Water spills all over the floor.)*

SIYI: Ting!

WENQING *(appeasing her):* Let them go.

SIYI: Mind your own business! *(To the outside):* Ting!

(Zeng Ting returns followed by a puzzled Miss Yuan. Zeng Ting looks at his mother.)

SIYI *(picks up a bowl of ginseng soup):* Drink this, your father doesn't want it.

YUAN *(looking surprised and envious):* Ginseng soup!

TING: I don't want it.

SIYI *(severely):* Drink it!

TING *(takes a sip and spits it out):* Really—it's spoiled.

SIYI: Nonsense! *(Takes it and tastes it, finds something wrong with it, and sets it down.)* Humph!

(Yuan Yuan waves playfully at Zeng Ting, then walks softly behind

*him and pushes him out of the room. Zeng Ting crosses the threshold
with Yuan Yuan only a step away.)*

SIYI *(suddenly):* Miss Yuan!

YUAN *(startled):* Huh? *(Turns her head.)*

SIYI: Come over here!

YUAN *(walks over):* What's the matter?

SIYI *(smiling):* We would like to invite you and your father to
  celebrate Midautumn Festival with us today. Have you told
  him?

YUAN *(with disdain):* You want to invite us for lunch?

SIYI *(flattering):* Ah yes, we especially want to invite this beautiful
  young lady, Miss Yuan.

YUAN *(innocently, bluntly):* That's a lie. You really want to invite
  Father and Miss Su. I know all about it.

SIYI: Who told you that?

YUAN *(arrogantly):* Uncle Jiang, the Gu Laoye told me so.

SIYI *(with a kind expression):* Well, wouldn't you like a new
  mother?

YUAN: I don't have a mother and I don't want one.

SIYI *(trying to persuade her):* It's good to have a mother. Wouldn't
  you like Miss Su to be your mother?

YUAN *(confused):* Me?

VOICE OF ZENG TING *(from the front courtyard):* Hurry up, Yuan
  Yuan, it's getting windy now.

YUAN *(suddenly takes out an envelope and shoves it at Siyi):* This is
  for you!

SIYI *(surprised):* What is it?

YUAN: Our rent. Father wanted me to give it to you. *(Runs out
  the living room door.)*

SIYI *(with disdain):* What an undisciplined child!

WENQING *(uneasily):* What are you and Jiang Tai up to? What do
  you two have in mind for Sufang?

SIYI *(rolling her eyes):* What do you mean? She has to get married
  sometime, doesn't she? She can't be an old maid and wait
  on the Old Master for the rest of her life, can she?

WENQING: She hasn't said anything about it. How do you know she wants to get married?

SIYI *(grinning slyly)*: Maybe you can't tell by looking at her, but I can guess. I didn't do any kind works in my last life, so in this one I think I should do some good for others. I hate to see her burying herself away.

WENQING: Marriage is of course a good thing. But to someone like Dr. Yuan, who does nothing but study dried-out skulls . . .

SIYI: What's it to you whom she marries? What are you so concerned about? *(Maliciously)*: Do you want to follow her, to be her maid as part of the dowry so that you can prepare her ink and paper? Or would you prefer to make her bed and be her "kept man" at night?

WENQING *(angry)*: What kind of a person are you? Talking behind people's backs like this?

SIYI *(also furious)* Nonsense! What kind of a person are *you*? You're the one who fancies another woman!

WENQING: She's an old maid and she's been in our home waiting on Father for so many years . . .

SIYI *(finally saying what's on her mind)*: That's exactly what I don't like—having an old maid like her living in our home, painting and writing and taking care of the Old Master all day long. And she acts as if she's the only intelligent person around.

WENQING *(sighs)*: At any rate, I'm going away. As long as Father agrees, you can all . . .

SIYI: He has no choice. First of all, we're so broke that we've even had to rent out the living room to strangers. And we can't afford to support relatives who don't work. *(Looks at him peevishly and disdainfully.)* And what's more, if she feels like getting married, who are you to . . .

WENQING *(fed up; impatiently)*: Who says I don't want her to get married? Who says so? Who says so?

SIYI *(suddenly realizes that Miss Su has entered through the small door*

of the study; she laughs cunningly like a cat that has seen a mouse):
I don't want to quarrel with you, my master. Miss Su is
here!

*Sufang is about thirty years old. She was born into a notable family in
southern China. Her father was a famous scholar who did not leave
much to the family after his death. Her mother also passed away shortly
after. After her parents died, Sufang was invited to stay with her mother's sister. Obeying her mother's will, she moved to Peking to live in
the Zeng family. Since then she has never returned to the South. She
was treated very well by old Mrs. Zeng before she died; and since the
old woman's death, Sufang has become a crutch to her uncle. Wherever
he goes, she goes along. This is especially true now that Zeng Hao is
getting on in years and his health is failing. Sufang is his only comfort.
Yet throughout these years nobody has really given serious consideration
to her future.*

*The first impression one has upon meeting her is her quietness.
Her reticence makes it almost impossible to detect all the pain and hopes
suppressed in her heart. Having lived with relatives for so many years,
she has developed an extraordinary tolerance—listening quietly to all
the sarcastic remarks directed at her. It is only through the exchange of
poetry and letters with Wenqing that she unconsciously reveals her
melancholy.*

*She conducts herself with natural grace. Her dress has a quiet
elegance. She is wearing an old navy-blue wool "qi pao" dress which is
slightly loose but fits her well.*

SIYI *(to Sufang, smiling broadly):* Do you see how nasty he is, Su
Meimei?[22] Here he is getting ready to leave and he's ranting
and raving at me like this. *(Goes into the same nonsense again.)*
Those who don't know me well might think that I've been
a real terror at home. Those who understand me know that
I'm nothing but a punching bag. Not only do I have to take

---

[22]Literally means "younger sister." The term, however, is often used to address
a younger woman in an intimate way.

his abuse *(pointing at Wenqing)* day in and day out, but I also have to put up with his father, his sister, and his brother-in-law. *(Self-pitying)*: Even my son and daughter-in-law are treating me poorly! *(Intimately to Sufang)*: You, Su Meimei, are the only one in this family who shows me any kindness and respect; you're the only one . . .

(Sufang does not quite understand what has brought on this flood of words, but manages to smile quietly.)

WENQING *(impatient with his wife, interrupts)*: Is Father up yet?

(Siyi stops talking. Silence immediately prevails in the room.)

SUFANG *(calmly)*: Uncle has been up for a long time. *(Sees the damaged painting on the floor and picks it up.)* Isn't this the painting that Cousin Wenqing did?

SIYI *(starts up again)*: None other. It's because his painting was chewed up by rats that he's making such a fuss so early in the morning.

SUFANG *(genuinely kind)*: Oh, it's not so bad, I'll mend it for him.

WENQING *(smiles apologetically)*: Oh don't bother, it's not worth all that trouble.

SIYI *(glances cynically at Wenqing with a simulated smile)*: Why don't you let Su Meimei fix it for you? *(To Sufang)*: After all, you two have been like a duet—one sings, the other harmonizes. Now that he's leaving, you should have something to remember each other by.

SUFANG *(detects her sarcasm; not knowing what to do with the painting, stammers)*: Then I . . . I'll . . .

WENQING *(trying to save her from further embarrassment)*: Why don't you go ahead and mend it then? It's a shame to let it go like this.

SIYI *(rolls her eyes)*: Oh it really would be a shame. *(Sighs to herself.)* I always wanted to have a pair of capable hands like Su Meimei's, good at needlework and at painting and calligraphy. *(Laughs affectedly.)* Want to hear something funny? Sometimes when I'm daydreaming, I imagine picking up a meat cleaver *(behind the smile is a spark of poison)*, and hacking off *(makes hacking gesture)* those talented hands and attaching them to myself.

SUFANG *(frightened)*: Oh! *(Draws back her pale hands.)*

WENQING: What kind of a joke is that?

SIYI *(laughs victoriously)*: I'm such a clumsy, crude woman, with a big mouth and no brains! *(Picks up Miss Su's hand and rubs it gently.)* Su Meimei, please don't mind me. I'm always so direct. I can never be graceful. I've often told Wenqing *(glances sideways at Wenqing)* that if I were a man I would never marry someone like me. *(Even more intimately)*: Don't you agree, Su Meimei? Don't you . . .

As Sufang struggles with her embarrassment and helplessness in searching for the appropriate response, Zeng Ruizhen—the wife of Zeng Ting and daughter-in-law of Siyi—enters hurriedly through the living room door. She is carrying a big package of sandalwood and a bundle of incense.

Zeng Ruizhen is only eighteen years old, but her tired face causes her to look much older. No one can believe that she is under twenty. As a result of living in this extremely oppressive environment, she has developed a hidden but strong rebellious attitude that is never evident to strangers. One can detect sadness, discontent, and bitterness in her eyes. She seldom smiles and does not possess the slightest hint of femininity. Against the advice of her mother-in-law, she wears neither makeup nor colorful dresses. On this account, she has been reprimanded repeatedly by Siyi.

Whenever she is scolded by her mother-in-law, she stares at her coldly, expressionless and indifferent. She would never shed tears in the presence of a person she detests. Though she is suffering deeply inside, she reveals no sign of weakness. When alone in her room and in despair over the thought of the lonely years ahead, she has contemplated suicide. On the other hand, she has reached the angry decision that she must leave this oppressive household and seek at all costs a new beginning for her life.

When she married Zeng Ting, she was only sixteen years old and had spent two years in secondary school. In retrospect, it seems as if she has been imprisoned in this cage for decades. In this scholarly family, she has been driven, in the shortest span of time, from a girl's natural naivete into the sadness and worries of womanhood. All the hardship she has suffered has changed her into a sad and reticent person, much to the surprise of her old friends. She and her young husband have nothing to talk about, and she does not want to lower herself by playing the subservient role of a daughter-in-law. She reluctantly fulfills the ceremonial obligations of a granddaughter-in-law in the Zeng family, but deep in her heart she knows that it will be impossible to remain in this environment for long.

In this gloomy family, Aunt Sufang is her only friend. Sometimes Ruizhen weeps quietly in front of her. Likewise she sympathizes with Auntie Su and shares her pain. Yet the two of them belong to different generations. Ruizhen has hope and has gradually come to realize that her future does not belong to this small world. Auntie Su's way of thinking, on the other hand, has prevented her from breaking away from the confines of the Zeng family. Ruizhen is fond of reading, and books have taught her about today's world outside. Through books she has also made some sincere friends who earnestly recommend new reading to her and help her to explore different aspects of life. Every now and then she will confide in Auntie Su about these matters, but the other members of the family are unaware of her new exposure to the world.

She does not look well these days. A sudden physical change in her body has stirred a fearful contradiction in her. She feels uneasy about the unborn child inside her and is keenly aware of her own misfortune in having to live aimlessly in this family. She cannot understand why she had to marry this boy and bear his child. Because of this predicament, she has been going out frequently, trying to find a solution to the problem.

She enters hesitantly, for she knows that the dark dress she is wearing will displease her mother-in-law.

RUIZHEN: Mother! Father!
SIYI (sarcastically): I'm surprised to see that it took only a phone

call to get you home. I was just talking to Auntie Su earlier about sending a car to pick you up.

RUIZHEN: I, I'm not feeling very well.

SIYI *(smirking)*: But isn't this your home? Don't you think I can take good care of you, my little mistress?

SUFANG *(on Ruizhen's behalf)*: Cousin Siyi, she hasn't been feeling well.

SIYI *(grudgingly)*: Are you feeling better now?

RUIZHEN *(softly)*: Yes.

SIYI *(glances at her spitefully)*: Then go. I'm afraid that you . . . Hurry up and go pay respect to the ancestors.

RUIZHEN: All right. *(Turns and walks toward the study.)*

SIYI *(beaming, to Sufang)*: I give in too easily, I'm simply not suited to be a mother-in-law. As soon as I see . . . *(Abruptly turns toward Ruizhen)*: Hey! Ruizhen, how can you leave without even greeting your father-in-law?

RUIZHEN: I did greet him.

SIYI *(displeased by Ruizhen's defiance; her mien darkening immediately, to Wenqing)*: Did you hear her? *(Without waiting for his answer, she turns at once to Ruizhen)*: I didn't.

RUIZHEN *(looks at her mother-in-law coldly, then turns to Wenqing)*: Father!

WENQING *(with pity for her)*: Run along now.

SIYI *(to Ruizhen)*: What about Auntie Su?

RUIZHEN *(mechanically)*: Auntie Su.

SIYI *(to Sufang, grinning slyly, seeming to be at once kind and nasty)*: Our Young Mistress really has no manners at all. *(To Ruizhen, pretending to be kind)*: You still haven't thanked Auntie Su. You know she really cares about you. It was she who telephoned you.

RUIZHEN: Thank you, Auntie Su.

SIYI: Do you know that Ting is back from school already?

RUIZHEN: I know.

SIYI: Did you see him flying the kite with Miss Yuan?

RUIZHEN *(softly)*: Yes, I did.

SIYI (*pointing at Ruizhen, she says to Sufang):* Have you ever seen such a fool? She knew! And she even saw them! (*Turns to Ruizhen suddenly):* Then why didn't you hurry back and keep an eye on him? (*Self-impressed, advising):* Don't be a fool. He is your man, your husband. He's your support for the rest of your life.

WENQING (*in a lonely tone):* They're only children, playing together. Why must you get so excited about it?

SIYI (*intentionally):* Who's excited? You always side with this kind of woman. (*Casts a glance at Sufang.*) I can always spot them. They'll do the lowest things to get a man. Ruizhen, go and prepare the ancestral altar, and tell Ting to stop fooling around with that crazy girl and get in here and put on his ceremonial jacket. It's time for him to pay respect to the ancestors too.

(*Ruizhen picks up a big bag of sandalwood and incense.*)

SIYI: Come back here. Who asked you to buy this sandalwood?

(*Ruizhen remains silent.*)

SUFANG (*softly):* Cousin Siyi . . .

SIYI (*pretends not to hear, still talking to Ruizhen):* Have you come into a fortune or something? Who told you to buy that big pile of junk? Who is that obnoxious busybody?

SUFANG (*calmly):* It was I, Cousin Siyi.

(*Silence. Ruizhen exits through the small door of the study.*)

SIYI (*laughs through the gloom):* Ah, really! Honestly, you know how I am. I say whatever's on my mind, but I don't mean to offend people. I'm as blunt as Zhang Fei,[23] can't keep my mouth shut. (*Feigns apology.*) Oh, if I had only known that it was your idea . . .

SUFANG (*calmly):* Uncle wanted it for his evening prayers.

WENQING: Father asked for it several days ago.

SIYI (*paying lip service):* Oh, our Old Master is such a fussbudget.

---

[23]Zhang Fei was a major figure in *The Romance of Three Kingdoms,* the famous novel written by Luo Guanzhong of the late Yuan and early Ming dynasties. General Zhang was characterized as brave but impulsive.

He's so hard to please. All he needed to do was to ask me to buy it for him. *(Intimately)*: Ah, Su Meimei, you just don't know how grateful Wenqing and I are to you. If you weren't here, I can just imagine how often the Old Master would lose his temper with me. *(In a concerned voice, softly)*: I supposed he was feeling ill again last night?

SUFANG *(nodding slightly)*: Yes.

SIYI *(satisfied, to Wenqing)*: You see, I was right. *(To Sufang)*: I heard the Old Master coughing, and I said to Wenqing, "the poor Old Master is having trouble breathing again" *(with a worried expression on her face)*. As soon as I heard him coughing I woke up and couldn't fall asleep again. I poked Wenqing and said, "Listen, here it's the middle of the night and Su Meimei has to go all the way down to the kitchen to fill the hot water bottle for Father. Really."

WENQING: What's bothering Father?

SUFANG *(weakly)*: His legs were bothering him and he wanted them massaged.[24] He also said that he's worrying about something.

SIYI *(interrupting)*: That must be . . .

WENQING *(grudgingly, to Sufang)*: So he asked you to massage him all night?

SUFANG *(with a sad smile)*: After a massage, Uncle can sleep a little better.

SIYI *(surprised)*: No wonder I saw you still massaging him early this morning.

WENQING *(sympathetically)*: In that case, you still haven't gone to bed yet.

SIYI *(talkatively)*: How could you stay up all night like that? *(Fondly)*: Why didn't you ask me to take over for a while? Good gracious, you'd better go to your room and get some sleep now. *(Ushering Sufang out.)*: You're frail enough as it is, how could you go a whole night without sleep? *(Feigning concern)*: How can I let you do this? Go and get some sleep,

---

[24]This kind of massage involves pounding gently with closed fists.

my dear little sister. If you get sick, I really wouldn't know what to do.

SUFANG *(sadly):* There's no need. I really couldn't sleep now.

SIYI: Wenqing, have you ever seen a more filial person than Su Meimei? I truly admire a person like Su Meimei. *(Flatters Sufang.)* She's quiet, friendly, kind, and always agreeable. *(Turns to Wenqing suddenly):* Wenqing, if I were a man, I'd marry a woman like Su Meimei and be happy for the rest of my life.

WENQING *(trying to rescue her):* Su Meimei, didn't you come to get ginseng soup for Father?

SUFANG: Oh, that's right.

SIYI: Why didn't you say so before? I had it ready long ago. *(Picks up the bowl of ginseng soup.)*

WENQING: Didn't Ting say that this soup was . . .

SIYI: Don't listen to Ting! Let me warm it up and bring it to him. *(Smiling.)* This is really a case of "the ugly woman meeting her parents-in-law." Even though she's ugly and they don't want to see her, it can't be helped. *(Starts out and then turns back.)* Oh, those two bowls of food in the kitchen . . . did you make them for Wenqing's trip?

SUFANG: Oh . . . yes.

SIYI *(needling):* Wenqing, see how lucky you are? Su Meimei is so good to you. It's the eve of your departure, and Su Meimei, who hasn't had a wink of sleep, has still gone to the trouble of making all this food for you. Aren't you even going to thank her? *(Smiles as she exits through the small door of the study.)*

(Silence; outside in the sky, the pleasant sound of the pigeons' whistles can be heard intermittently.)

WENQING *(regretful, with tears in his eyes, says softly):* Sufang . . . I . . . I . . .

(Sufang lowers her head and is silent.)

WENQING *(gazing at her, also lowering his head, says nervously):* Chen Naima, she has come to see us.

SUFANG *(controlling her grief):* She . . . she's in the front yard . . .

(Siyi suddenly comes in hurriedly through the small door of the study. Her head is visible in the doorway.)

SIYI *(her face full of smiles, waving her hand)*: Wenqing, Chen Naima is outside waiting for you. Since you're leaving soon, why don't you chat with her a bit. Come on, Wenqing!

(Sufang gazes at Wenqing, who lifelessly follows Siyi and exits through the small door of the study. The forlorn tune of the pigeons' whistles is heard. The single-wheeled water cart clatters monotonously on the pebbled street. From a distance, the cymbal of the blind fortune-teller creates a gentle, even tune. Fragments of the cold-drink hawkers' call, "Sour plum soup," are heard from the distant streets. Sufang stands still lost in thought. She suddenly sits down on a lone stool and starts sobbing softly. A breeze rattles the scrolls on the wall.)

VOICE OF YUAN YUAN *(playing with the kite outside; mixed with the clapping of hands)*: Fly, fly! Fly up high!

(Chen Naima enters, bringing Xiao Zhuer through the door of the main parlor which leads to the front yard. Xiao Zhuer stares back fixedly at the kite in midair. The sunlight shines straight into his rosy round face.)

CHEN: Miss Su!

XIAO *(uncontrollably claps his hands)*: Grandmother, look at the goldfish in the sky! *(Pointing outside the window at the sky, he cries regretfully)*: Oh, no! The goldfish is falling down again . . . the goldfish . . .

CHEN *(sees that Sufang is weeping alone, looks back at her grandson, and softly says)*: Don't yell. Go out and look.

(Xiao Zhuer is happily surprised; with a skip and a jump he goes outside. Naima silently walks to Sufang.)

CHEN *(slowly)*: What's wrong, Miss Su?

SUFANG *(lowers her head)*: Well, I . . . *(Sobs softly again. Momentary silence.)*

CHEN *(sighing, puts her hand on Sufang's slightly heaving shoulders)*: Miss Su, don't cry. I've been gone over half a year and when I come back, you're still crying?

SUFANG *(raises her head)*: I want to cry and let it all out. Naima, what kind of life is this? *(She throws herself onto the table and begins to cry.)*

CHEN *(lowering her head, almost in tears):* Don't cry. My dear Miss Su, last year I told you, I don't know how many times. *(Grievously):* Get married, that would be best for you. Even if you marry a widower. *(Simultaneously wiping away her tears and forcing herself to smile.)* Don't mind my being so frank. But how can a lady of your age live in your uncle's house for the rest of your life? *(Sufang begins to sob softly again.)* For better or worse, get married, my dear Miss Su. After all, this home can never be your own. *(Sufang begins to cry aloud.)*

CHEN *(in a low voice; secretly):* I was just in the front yard, and I took a peek at Mr. Yuan. He is actually quite a . . .

SUFANG *(sniffling):* Naima, please don't talk about this.

CHEN *(kindly):* All right, but have your horoscopes been matched?

SUFANG *(imploring her not to go on):* Please, Naima.

CHEN *(shaking her head):* Da Nainai is such an intolerant woman. My poor Master Wenqing has to take so much from her every day. Whenever I think of it, it hurts me so! *(Sorrowfully):* Ai! In this world nothing works out the way you want it to, you see. You and Master Wenqing, the two of you . . .

(Ruizhen hurriedly comes in from the small door of the study.)

RUIZHEN: Auntie Su, Grandfather wants you.

SUFANG: Oh. *(She gets up instantly, wipes her eyes, and walks to the study with her head lowered.)*

RUIZHEN: Grandfather is in the front room.

(Sufang, her head still lowered, turns around and walks toward the door to the living room. Ruizhen sees that she is crying and follows her.)

RUIZHEN *(in a low voice):* Auntie Su, you're . . .

(Sufang keeps on walking, with her head down.)

VOICE OF SIYI *(from backyard):* Ruizhen!

RUIZHEN *(stops and answers):* Yes!

VOICE OF SIYI *(from backyard, shrieking):* Where have you gone to, Ruizhen?

RUIZHEN: I'm here. *(She keeps on following Sufang.)*

SUFANG *(stops at the threshold of the living room)*: You'd better go!

RUIZHEN: No.

(Sufang walks on, both of them entering the living room. Sufang leaves from the door to the front yard. Siyi enters from the door of the study.)

SIYI: Ruizhen, you . . . *(Catches sight of Naima.)* Ah, Chen Naima *(face beaming, pointing to the backyard)*, hurry, your Master Wenqing has been looking for you everywhere!

CHEN *(excitedly)*: Ah, Master Wenqing, where is he?

SIYI: In the courtyard.

(Naima exits from the study happily but unsteadily. Ruizhen quietly walks through the living room door and approaches Siyi.)

RUIZHEN: Mother.

SIYI *(stares at her severely)*: Are you deaf? *(Looks around.)* I told you to call him. Where is he?

RUIZHEN: Well, I . . .

SIYI *(harshly)*: Out of my sight, you good-for-nothing!

(Ruizhen, with head lowered, walks past her.)

SIYI *(clenching her teeth)*: Look at you! *(Stamps her foot.)* Why don't you just drop dead!

(Ruizhen silently exits from the door of the study.)

SIYI *(simultaneously walking to the living room, calling)*: Ting . . . Ting!

(Zeng Ting enters from the door to the living room which leads to the front yard.)

TING *(his face perspiring)*: Mother.

SIYI *(coldly reprimands)*: Don't you know that I've been calling you?

TING *(apologetically smiles)*: Yes, I know.

SIYI *(anger diminishes)*: Hurry up and put on your jacket and gown and make your offerings to your ancestors.

(Zeng Ting immediately turns and heads toward the study.)

SIYI *(grabbing him, uncharacteristically kind)*: My child, don't go playing with that Miss Yuan any more; that wild girl has no manners at all. *(Half encouraging and half angry.)* If you don't think Ruizhen is good enough for you, I can get you another wife after you graduate from high school. In the meantime you have to study hard so your mother can be proud of you. In the future . . .

(As Zeng Ting is growing more impatient with her, Zhang Shun, the servant, enters from Jiang Tai's bedroom on the left-hand side. Zeng Ting seizes the opportunity and exits through the door of the study. As the door opens screams can be heard from the bedroom: "Get the hell out of here! Get out! Get out!" The door is slammed shut, closing off the sound of the screaming.)

SIYI: What's the matter, Zhang Shun?

ZHANG *(catching his breath):* Da Nainai, Zhang Shun would like to request an extended leave of absence.

SIYI: What's the matter this time?

ZHANG *(gesturing):* I can no longer wait on Gu Laoye. All day long he does nothing but pick on us servants and curse our ancestors for eight generations.

SIYI *(angrily):* He's like a mad dog. Don't pay any attention to him!

ZHANG *(cannot suppress his anger):* No, go find yourself another servant. Not only do I have to fend off all these collectors . . .

(Suddenly next door can be heard the shout, "That good-for-nothing!" A woman's voice crying: "Don't go in there, don't go." Male voice screaming: "Let go of me, I want to see her!")

SIYI *(with a sense of foreboding, she lowers her voice; to Zhang Shun):* Zhang Shun, let's go somewhere else and talk. Let him yell.

(Zhang Shun follows Siyi and both exit through the door of the study.)

The struggling Jiang Tai and his wife, Wencai, enter as the other two leave. Jiang Tai shakes her off, and she looks at him helplessly. Jiang Tai gestures angrily with a handful of cash.

Jiang Tai, the Gu Laoye, formerly studied chemistry abroad. When he came to Peking, he exploited the comfortable life-style there to the fullest and became rather debauched. His attitude and life-style are no different from those of the local playboys. He is about thirty-seven years old and has somewhat of a wasted look about him. Although he looks quite intelligent, he is not on a par with his more worldly peers. Consequently he tries to catch up by taking advantage of others in small ways; but in important matters he is usually the loser. Down deep he is not a bad person. After returning from abroad he had hoped to make something of himself. But for no apparent reason he gave up his profession and became a government official. He has held various posts, but has not been successful in any of them. In his last appointment he became involved in a major embezzlement scandal and had to resign in disgrace. He does not have much money left and has to live with his wife in his father-in-law's home. He complains constantly and vents his frustrations by drinking. The poorer he gets, the more ornery he becomes. He is often known to scream at people and to smash plates and bowls.

However, Jiang Tai also has his likable traits. He is straightforward, frank, and often fair. Yet he often abuses his ailing wife. On the rare occasions when her spirits lift and she says something that he does not agree with, he disdainfully asks, "What do you know?" He has another strong point: he knows everything about Peking's restaurants, theaters, and entertainment spots. Moreover, he is very particular about eating and is a known connoisseur. Not only does he have discriminating tastes, but he is also familiar with rare recipes. His descriptions are as convincing and as vivid as an essay by the famous writer Yuan Zicai. He loves to brag about his glorious past and about how his friends admired and adored him, unbelievable though it may seem.

He is always talking about mapping out his road to prosperity, but most of the plans remain on paper. This charade is merely to build his ego. Once, he decided to embark upon a venture manufacturing soap and put together a makeshift furnace in the deserted garden of the Zeng residence. On the first day he stirred up a huge caldron of thick yellow liquid that wound up looking like soft lumps of butter. It must have been the inadequacy of his chemistry textbook, which did not explain in full detail how soap is produced. Today the furnace and junk are piled in the deserted garden. No one ever mentioned the endeavor again.

After this failure he did not talk about striking it rich for awhile. But before long he could not resist whining to his wife in their own quarters: "One of these days, I'll invent a medicine like Tiger Balm Oil,²⁵ and then I'll be . . ." So he has many dreams of prosperity that will always remain dreams. His fortune-teller has proven inaccurate, for in the years during which he was supposed to get rich, nothing happened.

Recently he came up with a sudden brainstorm. He wants to get into business and has been trying to persuade his father-in-law to invest money in an export venture in Shanghai. He has also suggested that they sell the house and use it for capital. His father-in-law habitually refuses. But knowing his son-in-law's temper, he tries to evade the issue, hemming and hawing. As a result, Jiang Tai is most displeased.

He is a man of small stature with a wide forehead, full nose, and thick lips with a nice little moustache. He has restless eyes that complement his fidgety movements.

He is wearing a well-tailored brown suit of good quality; his tie is pulled halfway down. His hair is uncombed, and he looks generally untidy.

His wife, Zeng Wencai, is thirty-three. Ten years ago she was a great beauty, kind and demure. During her first few years of marriage, her husband was loving toward her. Later, she was often ill and lost her youthful beauty, becoming thin and frail. She is now even paler than the other members of the Zeng family and retains no trace of her past beauty. She is an extremely weak and indecisive woman. As a result of her traditional education, she worships her husband and caters to his every demand, accepting willingly his condescension and insults during the past several years. She has been ill for a long time and therefore enters unsteadily. Her lips are pale and her hair slightly disheveled. She is wearing a well-worn bluish-gray "qi pao" dress. Her green satin shoes are also worn.

---

²⁵Wan Jin You, or Tiger Balm Oil, is a kind of ointment that is considered a remedy for numerous minor ailments.

WENCAI (*begging Jiang Tai*): You can't do this! If you do this, how would it look?

JIANG (*furiously*): How would what look? I'm just going to give him this money. We live here, so we pay for our room; we eat their food, so we'll pay them for board.

WENCAI (*feebly*): Please don't shout like that. The servants will laugh behind our backs if they hear you.

JIANG (*angrily*): What's there for them to laugh about? We're going to move out of here after I pay them this. (*Waving the roll of bills in his hand, shouts in a rage*): Why didn't you give him the money when I told you to? (*Starts to go.*) I'm going to give this money to your father myself!

WENCAI (*holding on to him, trembling like a dying butterfly*): Jiang Tai, please don't embarrass me here, this is my father's home.

(*Siyi's face can be seen stretching out from the study door, trying to eavesdrop.*)

JIANG (*spits on the floor in disgust*): Your father's home! You'd find more good will in a hotel than here! (*Points at the backyard.*) If you take one penny from the old man when he dies, I'm going to divorce you just like that.

WENCAI (*appealing pathetically*): Where did you hear such horrible gossip? Who told you that my sister-in-law minded our staying here? And who ever mentioned that you're after your father-in-law's money?

JIANG (*arrogantly*): That's funny. Me? After that spare change? (*Angrily*): Listen here. The people in your family are all bloody fools! Peasants who have never seen real wealth! Worst of all is that sister-in-law of yours!

WENCAI (*nervously, in a low voice*): Don't shout like that. She may be in the next room.

JIANG (*lets himself go to his heart's content*): I'm shouting so that she can hear me. I want to see what she's going to do about it. I dare her to do anything! I'll kill her, I'll shoot her!

(Siyi, about to intrude, is sent backstage by that horrible threat.)

WENCAI *(sighing):* No matter what you say they're still our relatives.

JIANG: Relatives? *(Complaining.)* Relatives like this are dog shit! When I was rich and successful they all knew me. Now that I have no money and no job, all I get is dirty looks! *(Getting angrier.)* Good-for-nothings! Why don't you go and ask them, and see if they can remember borrowing money from me to buy land and property. It's because of them that I lost my job. And you think they care about that? Only yesterday I asked the old man to lend me three thousand dollars and wouldn't you know he . . .

WENCAI *(interrupting):* I'll talk to Father about that later!

JIANG *(angrily):* Oh no you won't! Don't embarrass me any further! You think your father is a kind man because he's a vegetarian and prays all day long? What he does is criminal! Here he has his own coffin, all lacquered and polished sitting in the house, and yet he still holds on to that old maid, and won't let her marry.

WENCAI *(weakly):* Stop that nonsense!

JIANG: Humph! *(Fiercely):* Now tell me, is he scared of dying or not?

WENCAI *(smiles dryly):* All old people are.

JIANG: Well, since he knows that he has to die soon, why is he being so choosy and objecting to everyone who tries to make a match for Miss Su?

WENCAI *(goodheartedly):* I suppose that's for her own good.

JIANG *(furiously):* Nonsense! He's selfish! Selfish! Selfish! The sooner I get away from this place the better! I'm getting out right now! I'm getting the hell out of here! I'm getting out!

(Zeng Ting enters through the study door.)

TING: Auntie, Uncle, Grandfather wants you to go and pay respect to the ancestors.

JIANG: I'm not going.

WENCAI: Ting, don't listen to him. We'll be there shortly.

TING: Mother says they're waiting for Auntie and Uncle to light the candles.

JIANG: I'm not going. I haven't even worshiped the ancestors of my own Jiang family.

WENCAI *(imploring):* Come on, please go and put on your ceremonial jacket!

(Sufang enters through the study door with a bag of infant's clothes in her hand.)

SUFANG *(looking around):* Do you know where Ruizhen is?

WENCAI: She's not here.

SUFANG *(to Jiang Tai):* You're still here, Cousin. Uncle's waiting for you in the ancestral hall!

WENCAI *(almost begging):* Please go, for my sake!

JIANG *(rolling his eyes):* Go tell him I don't have time for that. *(Exits through living room door that leads to the front yard, without turning his head.)*

WENCAI *(chasing after him):* Jiang Tai, stop. Listen to me. *(Exits.)*

(Zeng Ting is about to exit through the living room door.)

SUFANG *(begging sadly):* Ting, don't leave yet.

TING: Auntie Su.

SUFANG: You . . . *(unable to continue).*

TING: What's the matter?

SUFANG *(finally):* Why can't you and Ruizhen get along?

(Zeng Ting remains silent.)

SUFANG *(sadly):* You two are supposed to be husband and wife.

TING *(painfully):* Please don't bring that up again.

SUFANG: Suppose, suppose she were your sister, how could you be so cruel as to . . .

TING *(imploring):* Auntie Su, please!

(They sense someone approaching. As they turn to look they see Ruizhen entering hurriedly through the study door with her head lowered, hiding her sorrow.)

RUIZHEN *(surprised to see Zeng Ting there):* Oh, you, you're here too.

SUFANG (*instantly*): You two go ahead and talk. (*Hurriedly walks toward the living room.*)

VOICE OF YUAN YUAN (*from the front yard*): Zeng Ting, come on out!

(*Zeng Ting has nothing to say to Ruizhen to begin with. Now, hearing Yuan's call, he seizes the opportunity and hurries past Sufang toward the living room.*)

SUFANG: Ting, you . . .

(*Without turning, Zeng Ting exits through the living room door that leads to the front yard. Sufang turns and walks slowly up to Ruizhen, extreme sadness on her face.*)

RUIZHEN: Auntie Su! (*Starts to cry, holding onto Sufang.*)

SUFANG (*in a low, soothing voice*): Don't cry, Ruizhen.

RUIZHEN (*still sobbing*): I, I'm not, I'm not.

SUFANG (*holding her hand*): Why don't you go and lie down for awhile.

RUIZHEN (*shaking her head*): No. His mother wants me to help serve supper.

SUFANG (*worriedly, inquiring*): How come you went out so early today?

RUIZHEN: I had, I had something to take care of.

SUFANG (*touching her face, pityingly*): I think you should take a nap. Your eyes are all red.

RUIZHEN (*grievously*): No, his mother will say that I'm pretending to be sick again.

SUFANG (*sympathetically*): Are you still feeling nauseous?

RUIZHEN: I'm better now.

SUFANG (*unintentionally*): Ruizhen, let me tell them. It's better if I do it for you.

RUIZHEN (*resolutely*): No, no.

SUFANG: Then let's tell Ting.

RUIZHEN (*sadly*): What does he know? He's just a child.

SUFANG (*trying to persuade*): But why not tell him?

RUIZHEN (*shaking her head*): Auntie Su, you just don't understand.

SUFANG (*puzzled*): Why? (*With a look of joy.*) What is there to hide?

RUIZHEN *(looking painfully at Sufang):* Auntie Su, if only I could stay unmarried my whole life like you.

SUFANG *(quietly, sorrowfully gazing into space):* How can you be so childish?

RUIZHEN *(woefully):* But Auntie Su, we are children. At the end of the year I'll be eighteen and Zeng Ting is only seventeen. Somehow or other the two of us got thrown into this mess together. We hardly know each other; we have no feelings for each other. When we're in our room, we have nothing to say to each other. It's been going like this for two years, *(painfully)* and now . . . now this . . .

SUFANG *(kindheartedly):* But this will make your grandfather very happy.

RUIZHEN: Exactly, Auntie Su, and I want to know why. Why must we two pitiful creatures be forced into having more pitiful little creatures simply because Grandfather wants to have great-grandchildren?

SUFANG *(consoling):* People say it helps to have children; once a couple has children, their relationship improves.

RUIZHEN *(gravely shaking her head):* No, Auntie Su, I don't believe that. Things between us won't get any better. *(With certainty.)* Even if Zeng Ting treated me better, I couldn't go on living in a family like this. *(Disdainfully):* I'm even afraid to look my elders in the face. *(Takes Sufang's hand.)* Auntie Su, if you weren't here I would have killed myself a long time ago.

SUFANG *(moved):* Don't talk like that. You're still so young. All of us will be so happy when the baby comes.

RUIZHEN *(sorrowfully):* Auntie Su, how could anyone be happy here? We can't even pay the money we owe the Du family. Grandfather is even talking about selling the house . . .

SUFANG *(lowering her head, in agreement):* Yes.

RUIZHEN: The baby'll only add to the burden, and Zeng Ting hasn't even finished high school.

SUFANG (*smiling affectionately*): Now don't you go worrying like an old woman. If life's suffering isn't for our children, then what is it for? When the little one is born, I'll take care of him for you. I'll come and help you. Don't worry, when we come to the end of the road I still have some money that my mother left me. We can spend it on the baby.

RUIZHEN (*deeply moved*): Auntie Su, you are really . . .

SUFANG (*her eyes tear out of happiness*): Well then, Ruizhen, let me go and tell them the news about you. First I'll tell Cousin Siyi . . . she's so anxious to have a grandchild that she'll treat you much better than she does now.

RUIZHEN (*instantly*): No, no, you don't understand. I especially don't want her to know about it. No, don't, you mustn't tell them no matter what. (*Emotionally*): Auntie Su, you're the only one, only you . . . Oh, Auntie Su, I'm so confused. Last night I dreamt my mother was still alive and I was living like a little girl at home. (*Painfully*): Oh, Auntie Su, how wonderful it would have been if I had never grown up and gotten married!

SUFANG (*consoling her lovingly*): Don't cry, don't cry anymore. I've got something to show you! (*Opens the packages and shows her some beautiful woolen baby clothes.*) Ruizhen, do you think you can use these?

RUIZHEN (*staring at the dresses, dumbfounded*): Eh?

SUFANG: Do you like them?

RUIZHEN (*trembling*): You've made these already? (*Although slightly embarrassed, she cannot hide her smile.*) But, it's still early yet.

SUFANG: Oh, I can't really knit; I'm just learning.

RUIZHEN (*admiring the dresses one by one, happily*): Beautiful, beautiful, they're really beautiful. (*Suddenly sets them down.*) But Auntie Su, you don't even have enough money for yourself. How could you spend so much money on . . .

SUFANG: Because I love you and care about you. Ruizhen, you're not angry, are you? We've both lost our own parents and we're living in a house where we always have to live according to other people's wishes.

RUIZHEN (*lowers her head, holding firmly onto Sufang's hands*): Auntie Su. (*Tears roll down her cheeks.*)

SUFANG (*sadly but kindly*): You're about to become a mother, an adult. How would you even consider not having the baby? When the baby comes, Ting'll gradually learn to be nice to you. (*Wipes the tears off Ruizhen's eyes.*) Be nicer to him, he's just a little boy, you know. (*Shakes her head sorrowfully and sighs.*) You two are just children. You're eighteen and he's only seventeen. I can't blame you for not knowing about these things. (*Holds firmly onto Ruizhen's hands; sincerely*): Ruizhen, what you were talking about last night . . . you must never do it.

RUIZHEN (*in a low voice*): Why should we have this little thing? (*Gazing into space.*) He doesn't even like me.

SUFANG (*sincerely*): Ruizhen, the fact that Ting doesn't like you isn't the baby's fault. When you grow older, you'll think differently. No matter how difficult it is to have a child in the family, it still gives you something to hold on to. (*Stares at Ruizhen.*) Are you really going to listen to your girlfriends and run away to some strange place? Where can you go? (*Sadly*): Ai, where is our home, really!

RUIZHEN (*angrily*): I don't want a family, especially not this one.

SUFANG (*instantly presses on her hand, shaking her head*): No, you're still young. You don't understand what it's like to be a woman without a family of her own. (*Gently*): Always feeling lonely inside. (*Cannot control herself.*) Ever since I was a little girl . . (*Suddenly manages to suppress her own sorrow, turns swiftly, and says with a painful expression on her face*): Ruizhen, listen to me, you can't do a thing like that. You can't get rid of the baby.

RUIZHEN: No.

SUFANG: Did you go see that dreadful doctor again?

(Ruizhen is silent.)

VOICE OF WENQING *(from the backyard)*: Ruizhen!

SUFANG: Tell me the truth.

RUIZHEN *(looking at Sufang)*: Yes.

VOICE OF WENQING *(from the backyard)*: Ruizhen!

SUFANG: Then don't ever go back there again.

RUIZHEN *(painfully)*: No, I won't.

SUFANG *(sincerely)*: Promise?

(As Ruizhen nods slightly, Wenqing enters through the study door, his head lowered.)

WENQING *(startled, as he raises his head and sees Sufang)*: Oh, you're here! *(To Ruizhen)*: Ruizhen, go and fetch my jacket.

RUIZHEN: Yes, Father! *(Enters Wenqing's bedroom.)*

(Momentary silence; Sufang and Wenqing face each other without exchanging a word.)

WENQING *(lets out a long sigh)*: Sufang, I'm leaving soon. From now on, there there'll be no one for you to . . .

(Suddenly Yuan Yuan runs in happily through the living room door that leads to the front yard.)

YUAN *(calling)*: Uncle Zeng, Uncle Zeng!

WENQING *(smiles as he turns toward Yuan Yuan)*: What is it?

YUAN: Xiao Zhuer said that his grandmother brought you a pair of beautiful pigeons.

WENQING *(points at the pigeon in the cage)*: There it is.

YUAN *(picks up the cage)*: But there's only one in here?

WENQING *(painfully)*: The other one flew off when they were bringing it here.

YUAN *(appreciatively pointing at the pigeon in the cage; in a naive manner)*: Does it have a name?

WENQING *(nodding leisurely)*: Yes.

YUAN *(excitedly)*: What is it?

WENQING *(solemnly)*: It, it's called "Solitude."

YUAN: It's beautiful! *(Begging)*: Uncle Zeng, can I have it?

WENQING: All right.

YUAN *(joyously)*: Oh, thank you Uncle Zeng! You're really a great uncle! (*Picks up the pigeon cage and dashes off.*) Xiao Zhuer! Xiao Zhuer! (*Calling as she exits through the living room door that leads to the front yard.*)

(*Silence. Only the pigeons' whistles can be heard.*)

WENQING (*musters up his strength*): Thank you for the painting.

(*Sufang, with her head lowered, remains silent.*)

WENQING (*pulls out a fine sheet of paper from his pocket; slowly*): I composed several little verses for you last night. (*Shyly hands it over to her.*) Here, here they are.

(*Sufang takes it into her hands.*)

WENQING (*tenderly and sincerely*): Read them later.

SUFANG (*looking at him*): I don't think I can see you off later.

(*Siyi suddenly enters through the study door.*)

SIYI (*surprised*): Oh, I didn't know you two were in here. (*To Sufang*): The Old Master wants you.

SUFANG (*still unaffected by Siyi's intrusion, holds onto the paper*): Oh. (*Instantly walks to the study.*)

SIYI (*catches sight of the piece of paper she is holding and rolls her eyes*): Oh, my, there's another sheet of paper on the floor.

SUFANG (*unconsciously looks around*): Oh?

WENQING (*puzzled*): Where? (*Anxiously searches the floor with his eyes.*)

SIYI (*laughing ruthlessly*): Oh, there it is (*looking at Sufang*), it's in your hand!

VOICE OF OLD MASTER ZENG HAO (*from outside, wearily*): Sufang.

SUFANG: Yes? (*Exits through the study door.*)

SIYI (*her face darkens*): What's going on behind my back this time?

WENQING (*apprehensively*): What? . . . oh, nothing.

SIYI: What did you just give her?

WENQING (*denying*): Nothing.

SIYI (*severely*): You liar. You think you can hide it from me? Well, tell me then, what was in her hand? Tell me . . .

WENQING: I . . .

(*Ruizhen enters from bedroom on the right-hand side with the jacket.*)

RUIZHEN: Father, your jacket. (*Wenqing takes the jacket from her.*)

SIYI *(disgusted at Ruizhen)*: Get going. Your Auntie Su is waiting for you.

(Ruizhen exits through the study door. Wenqing puts on his jacket in silence.)

SIYI *(nagging)*: I've been a generous person my whole life and as a result I've been taken advantage of time after time. I don't care what kind of a game you two are playing behind my back. *(Changes her tone to that of the accepting and tolerant wife.)* After all, you can hardly call this a family. As the saying goes: "When the tree falls, the monkeys scatter." After the house is sold, you can either live with your son and daughter-in-law or you can go away with your darling little Su Meimei. As for myself, I plan to enter a nunnery outside the city and retire from the world. There I'll find peace. *(Fears that he does not believe her.)* And don't think I'm just saying that. I've already picked out a nunnery and made the arrangements with the head-nun there.

WENQING *(although he sees through this charade, he cannot help but get angry and says in a quivering voice)*: What is the point of this? What is the point of this?

SIYI *(complaining)*: After all, I've raised a son for the Zeng family. I've had my share of hardships. I don't owe this family anything. After Midautumn Festival, tomorrow, I'm going to hand the household over to your sister and move into the nunnery. *(Walks toward the bedroom.)*

(Zhang Shun enters hurriedly through the living room door that leads to the front yard.)

ZHANG *(out of breath)*: Da Nainai, the collectors from the coffin shop . . .

SIYI: Tell them to go talk to the Old Master.

ZHANG *(desperately)*: But Da Nainai, they insist on talking to you . . .

SIYI *(rolls her eyes)*: Tell them that Da Nainai just died. She just took her last breath. *(Enters her bedroom.)*

(Wenqing stares at the bedroom door. Zhang Shun sighs as he exits through the living room door leading to the front yard.)

WENQING: Siyi! *(Pushing on the bedroom door.)* Open up! What are you doing in there?

VOICE OF SIYI *(from inside, angrily):* I'm hanging myself.

WENQING *(pounding on the door):* Open the door! Open up! What are you doing? Tell me, what are you going to . . . *(Turns and looks and says in a low voice):* Here comes Father!

Zeng Hao enters through the study door, accompanied by Ruizhen, Sufang, and Chen Naima.

Zeng Hao looks no more than 65 years of age; he has frosty white hair and a puffy, yellowish face. He looks frail and sickly, has a sparse, grayish moustache and dull eyes which are always watering. Only when he boosts his energy for a discussion does he manifest the air of elegance characteristic of the Zeng children. He is miserly, selfish, and terrified of dying. He spends the entire day taking fortifying potions and believes in prescriptions that claim to prolong life. He has spent the past few decades living comfortably off the family inheritance, occasionally going to different areas to assume government posts, all of which have been sinecures. He would inevitably leave his position after a short time to return to the comforts of home and Peking. But now things are drastically different, as he feels the effect of fast-diminishing family wealth. His children are his biggest disappointment. Much of the family property has been sold, and now very little remains. Not having any skill or ability, he feels frustrated and worried. Yet he continues to cling to the superficial rituals and mannerisms of aristocratic tradition, which he considers absolutely essential for the education of children in an enlightened family. Every so often he boasts of his importance as head of the family, but deep down he is a bit leery of his daughter-in-law Zeng Siyi. Although Siyi observes all the superficial courtesies that he merits as the eldest member of the family, he is never quite sure what she is thinking. He also despises the arrogance and abrasiveness of his son-in-law—his incessant quarrels and his foolish schemes for getting rich. Old Master Zeng never used to mention his wealth, but then again, he also never mentions how badly off he has been lately. Crying poor would get his son-in-law off his back, but it would not be worth his daughter-in-law's reaction to a blatant confession of poverty. She, after all, has the household under her thumb. Until now his daughter-in-law has not dared to exhibit disrespect to his face. Yet he is fearful of how his children might treat him should they learn that he is leaving them nothing.

Of course, we may attribute the concern to his overly sensitive nature, but he actually is poverty-stricken. As far as he is concerned, this poverty will inevitably threaten his status as the head of an enlightened family. At times he doubts whether all that education has actually had any influence on his children. The safest course for him at this time is to "tolerate" the attitudes of his family members. However, the "tolerance" is having a disquieting effect on him. He cannot help complaining, at times incessantly. But most of the time, he simply pretends that he is oblivious to the whole situation. His needs are actually quite simple. Except for his medicine and his concern over the lacquer on his coffin, he tries not to be a burden to his children. Most of the time, he is content to stay in his room, practicing calligraphy and reading sutras. In such a way he avoids spending money as well as energy. When years of pent-up frustration cause him to lose his temper occasionally, he cannot be as feisty as he was in his prime.

He complains constantly, as if accusing others of committing innumerable injustices against him. He reprimands his children for their lack of filial piety and for their worthlessness; he bemoans the decline of the family fortune. He criticizes his neighbors [who are nouveau-riche] as crass and impolite; but ironically, the traditional refinement and culture of this declining scholarly family—the only source of his pride—are quickly vanishing.

He is not always aware of his selfishness. As is the case with Sufang, he believes that he is protecting a helpless orphan. Actually, Sufang pities him, protects him in her silent way, and shelters him from countless tribulations, large and small. Whenever he senses a weak moment in her, he suddenly becomes helpless and is beside himself. Aiming to touch her deepest sentiments, he unconsciously exaggerates his plight as a helpless, weak, and suffering old man, thus guaranteeing her lifelong slavery to him. He is constantly absorbed in self-pity. Thus, he is unaware of the suffering of others around him.

He is wearing a long, dark brown gown, loose and comfortable.

Over it he wears a soft, light jacket which Sufang made for him. Even though he says he is extremely sensitive to the cold, the jacket is open at the throat. He is wearing a pair of Western-style felt slippers. The bottoms of his pants are tied with gray satin ties. He is carrying a string of exquisite Buddhist prayer beads.

Sufang and Ruizhen are supporting him on either side at the elbows. Chen Naima stands next to them with a covered bowl in her hands.

HAO (*eyes closed, as if listening; nods his head*): Yes, yes.
WENQING (*uneasily*): Father.
(*Zeng Hao is lost in thought, and does not seem to hear. Chen Naima is smiling and talking. Everyone becomes still for a moment and listens to her.*)
CHEN (*excitedly, to Sufang*): The way I figure it, it's been fifteen years now, hasn't it? (*To Zeng Hao*): They've been lacquering this coffin for fifteen years! (*With envy and amazement*): My oh my. How many coats of lacquer does it have now?
HAO (*contented*): Over a hundred. (*Supported by them, he walks toward a long, narrow table.*)
CHEN: No wonder it's almost three inches thick. (*Illustrates with her fingers; puts down covered bowl.*)
(*Siyi comes out of the bedroom. Her face is beaming peacefully, as if she has forgotten all about the recent suicide threat.*)
SIYI: Father is here. (*She hurries over to help support him.*) Come sit here, Father, it's more comfortable. (*She helps Zeng Hao over to the sofa on the other side. Hurriedly to Ruizhen*): Ruizhen, move the other lounge over here. (*Helps Zeng Hao sit down. To Wenqing*): Aren't you going to bring some cushions over?
WENQING: Why yes, of course! (*Goes to the study to get the cushions and Ruizhen follows.*)
HAO (*eyes closed, fondling Buddhist prayer beads*): Give it another four or five years of lacquering, and then maybe it will be ready for me to rest in. (*Ruizhen comes out of the study with the cushions.*)

SIYI (*affectionately, pointing*): Put them behind him, young lady. (*As if dissatisfied with the way Ruizhen places the cushions, she bends over.*) Eh, let me do it. (*To Ruizhen*): Go and get a blanket and cover up your grandfather.

HAO (*opens his eyes*): Don't bother. (*Again closes his eyes and meditates.*)

SIYI (*more humbly*): Do you feel better now?

HAO: I'm all right.

WENQING (*walks forward*): Father.

HAO (*slightly nodding*): Uh. (*Pretends to be surprised.*) Oh, you haven't left yet?

SIYI (*glancing at Wenqing; then to Hao*): Wenqing will be leaving in a little while.

HAO (*to Wenqing*): Have you kowtowed to your ancestors?

WENQING: No.

HAO (*displeased*): Go! Go! Hurry up. Go and pay respect to the ancestors. Then we'll talk. (*Starts coughing.*)

WENQING: Yes, Father. (*Walks toward the door of the study.*)

CHEN (*has another opportunity to talk with Wenqing*): Master Wenqing, I'll keep you company. (*Both Wenqing and Naima exit from the door of the study.*)

HAO: Sufang, go and fetch my spittoon.

(*Sufang is about to turn to go into the study when Siyi speaks.*)

SIYI (*instantly smiling*): Don't trouble, Cousin Sufang, there's one in my room. Ruizhen, go get it for your grandfather. (*She brings the covered bowl of tea to Zeng Hao.*) Father, have some tea!

(*Ruizhen enters Siyi's bedroom. Zeng Hao rinses his mouth with the tea. Sufang hands over a spittoon, and Zeng Hao spits into it.*)

HAO: There's such a bitter taste in my mouth. (*Closes his eyes again.*)

SUFANG: Are you still feeling dizzy?

HAO (*glances at her and again closes his eyes, half talking to himself*): Dizziness and this bitter taste are signs of a bad liver! No wonder my chest is congested and full of phlegm. *(Slowly rubs his chest.)*

SIYI *(attentively):* I think we ought to have a Western-trained doctor look at you.

HAO *(opens his eyes, disgusted):* Whose idea is that?

SIYI: Or we could have Zhang Shun call in Dr. Luo?

HAO *(opens his eyes, shakes his head):* Dr. Luo uses ancient prescriptions from the Tang dynasty. They have very strong side-effects, and for someone of my age in my condition, they're . . . *(Unwilling to continue, sighing, he closes his eyes and coughs lightly.)*

(Ruizhen enters from Siyi's bedroom, handing a small spittoon over to Zeng Hao. He spits out another mouthful of phlegm into it, and then holds the spittoon.)

SIYI: The Du family sent their bookkeeper over again to collect the fifty thousand dollars.

HAO: Oh?

SIYI: Also, the cost of lacquering the coffin this year . . .

HAO *(irritated):* Money, money, all my life I've worked like a slave and when I'm sick I have to worry about it!

(Siyi's face darkens. Momentary silence.)

SUFANG *(consoling):* This year the coffin was lacquered especially well.

HAO *(does not want to embarrass Siyi further; nods in acknowledgment as his face brightens a little):* Yes, yes, maybe—maybe next spring we'll add a couple more coats of Sichuan lacquer to it, and then we can figure out how to pay off all our debts to the Dus. Then I'll feel I've closed my accounts for this life. *(Sighs unconsciously and looks at Ruizhen.)* If I'm really lucky, I'll be a great-grandfather next year.

SIYI *(breaks into a big smile):* Oh yes! When we were kowtowing to the ancestors a while ago, I asked Ruizhen to say a special prayer for children. Hopefully the ancestors will have mercy on her so that she can give you a great-grandson soon.

HAO *(wrinkles of laughter begin to surface on his puffy face):* Ruizhen, did you pray for it?

(Ruizhen lowers her head and remains silent.)

SIYI *(nudging her and in a sharp tone):* Your grandfather asked you whether you prayed for it or not?

(Ruizhen turns her back on her.)

SUFANG *(urging her):* Ruizhen!

RUIZHEN *(turns toward Zeng Hao):* Yes, Grandfather, I did.

HAO *(smiles, satisfied):* That's good.

VOICE OF WENCAI *(from outside):* Jiang Tai! Jiang Tai!

SIYI *(mumbling):* Just look at this child. Now what are you crying about?

(Wencai and Jiang Tai enter through the living room door leading to the front yard, pushing and shoving.)

WENCAI *(pleading):* Jiang Tai! Jiang Tai! *(Pulling him in.)*

JIANG *(mutters angrily as he enters):* All right! All right! I'm coming! You don't have to drag me!

(All turn in their direction as they approach.)

HAO: What's the matter?

WENCAI: Father! *(Turns to Jiang Tai; in a low voice):* Just kneel down and kowtow. You don't have to change your clothes.

SIYI *(makes fun of Jiang Tai intentionally):* Your son-in-law is here to pay his respects to you, Father, on Midautumn Festival.

HAO *(thinking that Jiang Tai is going to kowtow to him, bends forward and makes a gesture to help him up):* Oh! You needn't do that! Please—why all this fuss?

(Jiang Tai looks at Siyi with a scowl. As Zeng Hao is bending forward, about to stand up, Jiang Tai hesitantly makes a half bow to the old man and then sits down first.)

JIANG *(looks around the room as he waits for Zeng Hao to sit down again; then immediately):* I have something to say. *(Points at his bedroom.)* That wall outside my room is just about to collapse! Are you people going to fix it or not?

WENCAI *(nervously in a low voice):* What's the matter now?

JIANG *(to Wencai):* Don't interfere! *(Turns to Siyi and Zeng Hao):* Are you going to fix it? If not, I'm going to get my things together and get the hell out of here!

HAO *(not knowing what is going on):* What?

SIYI *(gently, but making sure that she gets the stern message across to him)*: Gu Laoye, you don't understand. I would never think of not fixing it, but I heard that Father wants to sell the house and start a business, so . . .

HAO *(displeased)*: Sell the house?

SIYI: To our neighbors, the Du family.

HAO *(slightly angry)*: Says who! Who told you that?

SIYI *(glances over to Jiang Tai, smiles sarcastically)*: Let's see . . . who could it have been?

JIANG *(about to explode)*: I said it. *(Stares at Zeng Hao disdainfully.)* And I don't remember who the liar was who told me in the first place.

HAO *(unable to tolerate all this in his own house)*: Jiang Tai, is this how you talk to your elders?

JIANG: All right, I'm leaving. *(Gets up and starts to walk away.)*

WENCAI *(softly, almost in tears)*: Jiang Tai, sit down now.

SUFANG *(pleading)*: Cousin!

(Jiang Tai, being subtly restrained, sits down reluctantly. Silence. During this time, Wenqing enters quietly from the study, and stands to one side.)

HAO *(stares at Wenqing for a moment and says in a trembling voice)*: All right, I said it, I said it. I had to do it for the sake of this whole bunch of worthless children. We're going through hard times now, and there's not a single one of you who's earning any money *(glances angrily at Wenqing)* . . . and my oldest son is a loafer! The Du family next door is after us daily to pay our debts and is pressing us to sell our house. But are we going to hand over our house to them just like that, just because they offer ten or twenty thousand? *(Gets angrier as he speaks.)* This nouveau-riche textile manufacturer is taking advantage of us; he thinks money can buy anything. He even sent someone to buy the coffin I've been lacquering for fifteen years. *(Shaking in anger.)* People like that are so uncivilized! How can I let them have the very coffin I'm going to be laid to rest in? *(To Wencai)*: Say something, Wencai. *(To Wenqing):* You're the oldest, Wenqing, you say something! *(Wenqing lowers his head.)* You are my son . . .

(Chen Naima enters through the study door.)

CHEN *(happily):* Master Wenqing! *(Seeing that Siyi is pointing at Zeng Hao and signaling at her to stop by waving her arm, she falls silent abruptly and sneaks out through the living room door.)*

HAO: This house was handed down to us by our ancestors. Every blade of grass, every tree here now comes out of blood and sweat of Jingde Gong, who started with nothing. We eat here, we live here, from youth to old age. We have depended on this little blessing our ancestors gave us so that we don't have to worry about food and shelter. *(Pounds the arm of the sofa.)* Maybe you people don't appreciate this, but how do you think I could sell the house to this nouveau-riche family, sell it to this kind of . . .

JIANG *(raises his hand):* Listen, leave me out of this. I have never given a damn about your selling this house.

HAO *(taken aback briefly by what Jiang Tai said, and continues angrily):* This upstart textile manufacturer, this scoundrel who would be so low as to buy someone else's coffin, this . . .

(Suddenly a deafening sound of firecrackers can be heard from next door.)

HAO *(flabbergasted):* What's that? *(Tries to get up, as if overwhelmed by the excitement.)* What is that? What is it?

SUFANG *(tries to scream in the midst of the noise):* Don't worry, they're only setting off firecrackers!

HAO *(covers his ears, excitedly):* Close the door, close the door!

(Wenqing and Ruizhen rush to the folding door of the living room and close it. The sound of firecrackers fades, but continues for a while.)

WENCAI *(sighs deeply amid the noise):* Whose family is setting off all those firecrackers?

JIANG *(grins sarcastically):* Humph! Isn't that the nouveau-riche Du family?

HAO *(shakes his head):* Look at them! They make such a great fuss over Midautumn Festival you'd think they were marrying off their daughter.

(Chen Naima enters through the living room door.)

CHEN *(clapping her hands, laughing):* Miss Su, that family is so funny! The daughter calls her father "old ape," and the father calls the daughter "little monkey." And there's also a strange thing that looks like a wild gorilla sitting in their room. While the old ape draws pictures, the little monkey climbs all over him. *(Bends forward and backward, as she cannot control her laughter.)* They're going to turn the room upside down . . .

HAO *(puzzled):* Who's that?

CHEN: Who else but Mr. Yuan and his daughter? I think Mr. Yuan is a nice person. He laughs all day long for no reason at all.

SIYI: Chen Naima, why don't you go into the kitchen, see if everything is ready, and then set the table. The Old Master invited Mr. Yuan to lunch in honor of Miss Su!

CHEN: Oh, oh, yes, yes! *(Happily exits through the living room door.)*

SIYI *(brings a serious matter to Zeng Hao's attention):* I hear that Mr. Yuan will be leaving in a few days. I wonder how you feel about Su Meimei marrying . . .

HAO *(shakes his head disdainfully):* I think this fellow . . . *(Jiang Tai, who knows exactly what is on Zeng Hao's mind, grunts contemptuously. Hao glances over at Jiang Tai, and says angrily to Sufang, who is about to leave the room):* All right, Sufang don't go yet. Since you're here now we can all discuss this matter.

SUFANG: I have to go and make your medicine.

JIANG *(with good-natured sarcasm):* Ah, my dear Miss Su, haven't you made enough medicine for a lifetime? *(Rapidly says):* Sit down, sit down, sit down, sit down.

(Sufang sits down reluctantly.)

HAO: Sufang, how do you feel about this?

(Sufang lowers her head in silence.)

HAO: Su, tell me what's on your mind? Don't worry about me

. . . just think of yourself. This uncle of yours won't be able to take care of you for long. But the way I look at it this fellow Mr. Yuan . . .

SIYI *(hastily)*: Oh yes, Su Meimei, you really have to take this seriously, you mustn't continue disregarding your uncle's best intentions. Later, you may regret wasting your life away . . .

HAO *(also interrupts hastily)*: Siyi, why don't you let her think for herself? This is a once-in-a-lifetime decision, so she should make up her mind herself. *(Fakes a smile.)* We can only offer her our advice. Sufang, tell us, what do you think?

JIANG *(cannot control himself any longer)*: What's the matter here? Mr. Yuan isn't a horrible monster! He's a scholar, an anthropologist. First of all he's a good person and second he's well-educated; what's more, he has an income. It, it only seems right that . . .

HAO *(calm and controlled)*: No, no, why don't you let her think for herself? *(Turns to Sufang anxiously)*: Sufang, you have to understand, you are my only niece, and I've always treated you like my very own daughter. Wouldn't I keep on taking care of my own daughter if she didn't want to get married?

SIYI *(interrupting)*: That's right, Su Meimei, daughters who can't find husbands aren't . . .

(Wenqing, who cannot bear to listen to this any longer, starts walking toward the study.)

SIYI *(stares at Wenqing from the corner of her eyes; wickedly)*: Where are you going? Where are you going?

(Without turning back, Wenqing exits through the study door.)

HAO: What's wrong with Wenqing?

SIYI *(smiles sarcastically)*: He probably went to prepare your medicine! *(Turns to Sufang affectionately)*: Don't worry, Su Meimei. We brought this up because we care about you. No one'll spread gossip around even if you spend the rest of your life here in the Zeng family. *(Maliciously)*: Who wouldn't take care of a daughter who doesn't marry? What's more, Su

Meimei, your parents are dead, and you have no close relatives . . .

HAO (*knows what she is insinuating and interrupts without waiting for her to finish*): Enough, enough, Da Nainai, you can keep all that kindness to yourself.

(*Siyi's face suddenly turns sullen.*)

HAO (*turning to Sufang*): Well, Sufang, have you made up your mind?

SIYI (*to Sufang anxiously*): Tell us!

WENCAI (*has been listening and nodding in agreement all along; suddenly says kindly*): Go ahead, Su Meimei, I think . . .

JIANG (*to his wife, abruptly*): You keep quiet!

(*Wencai is silent as Sufang quietly gets up and heads for the living room door.*)

HAO: Sufang, say something, my little lady. You should at least let us know your opinion.

SUFANG (*shakes her head*): I, I have no opinion. (*Exits through the living room door.*)

HAO: Ai, how can you not have an opinion on such a matter?

JIANG (*growing intolerant*): Do you people mind if I say something?

HAO: What?

JIANG: If you want to hear what I have to say, fine. If not, I'm leaving right now.

HAO: All right, go ahead. Of course you can say what's on your mind.

JIANG (*frankly and directly*): In that case, I think you should all leave Sufang alone. Can't you see something's bothering her? Why do you go on bickering and insulting a poor, lonely old maid like her? Why . . .

SIYI: Insult her?

WENCAI: Jiang Tai.

JIANG (*outraged*): You certainly were insulting her. She's been working so hard for all these years waiting on the old and the young, the living and the dead, the Old Master, the

Young Masters, the Old Mistress, the Young Mistress. She's been taking care of this family all along. And now she's over thirty, and yet you still want to hold on to her, you won't let her go, what are you trying to do?

HAO: You . . .

WENCAI: Jiang Tai!

JIANG: Do you want her to follow you into the coffin too? To have her burned to ashes and sacrificed to your ancestors? Shouldn't we listen to our consciences? I'm leaving now; here's a letter *(pushes a letter into Zeng Hao's lap)* for you to read.

WENCAI: Jiang Tai!

(Jiang Tai stalks out of the parlor angrily, and exits through the living room door.)

HAO *(displeased)*: What, what's the meaning of this? I, I have never heard such nonsense in my life.

(Simultaneously opens the envelope with shaking hands, revealing some banknotes and a small piece of paper. While Zeng Hao is reading the letter, Zhang Shun enters quietly with some bowls and chopsticks in his hands. Ruizhen goes over to help him move the tables and chairs noiselessly. They set the table.)

HAO *(reads through the letter quickly and is furious)*: What's the meaning of this? *(He raises his arm, with banknotes in his hand.)* He wants to pay me rent? *(To Siyi)*: Siyi, what's this all about?

SIYI *(grins sarcastically)*: I don't know what's wrong with him.

WENCAI *(already on her feet reading the letter, pleads nervously)*: Father, please don't pay any attention to him. He has been so unhappy the past few years . . .

HAO *(angrily)*: Let's forget about Jiang Tai. He may be my son-in-law, and supposedly my half-son, but he is not a real Zeng. *(To Wencai)*: But you're my daughter, so you should know that the Zengs are a cultured family. Scholarship always comes first, and no one ever worries about money. If the two of you want to stay here, fine. But if you don't, that's fine with me too. No matter what, there's no need to talk about paying room and board to your father . . .

WENCAI *(sobbing)*: Father, just pretend you never had me as your daughter . . .

HAO *(shaking in anger)*: Uh, uh, nobody is going to walk around the Zeng family showing off his money! Not in the Zeng family!

WENCAI *(bursts into tears, as she cannot bear to hear her father's reprimands)*: Oh, Mother, why did you have to die and leave me here. Oh my Mother!

SIYI: Gu Nainai!

(Wencai, still weeping, runs into her own bedroom.)

HAO *(lets out a deep, long sigh)*: Bunch of good-for-nothings! Can't even talk to them anymore. Serve supper now, Zhang Shun, and invite Mr. Yuan over.

(Zhang Shun exits through the living room door. Wenqing enters through the study door.)

WENQING: Father!

HAO: Are you leaving?

WENQING: I'm going to take the one o'clock train.

HAO: Have you stopped smoking that opium of yours?

WENQING *(lowers head)*: Yes, I have.

HAO: You really have?

WENQING *(ashamed, blushes)*: Yes, really.

HAO: How about cigarettes.

WENQING *(lowers his head)*: I've quit smoking those too.

HAO *(stares at Wenqing's nicotine-stained fingers)*: Don't lie to me. *(Scolds.)* Look at those smoke-stained fingers of yours. *(Sighs as he shakes his head.)* Look at you. How, how can you find work looking the way you do?

WENQING *(examines them without realizing it)*: I, I'll wash them later.

HAO: Where's Ting?

SIYI *(instantly runs to the living room door that leads to the front yard and calls)*: Ting! Your grandfather wants you.

HAO: What's he doing?

WENQING: I think he's flying kites with Miss Yuan.

HAO: Flying kites! Instead of studying the *Zhao Ming Anthology* he's flying kites!

WENQING: Ting!

VOICE OF A SCREAMING ZENG TING *(in the living room):* Stop! My grandfather's in there! My grandfather's inside!

VOICE OF A ROWDY YUAN YUAN: Just try and get away! Just try and get away!

(The folding door of the living room is thrown open. Zeng Ting rushes in, still yelling; a sweaty Yuan Yuan follows, carrying an empty bucket in one hand, and holding a string of lighted firecrackers in another. They are followed by Xiao Zhuer, who has a stick of burning incense in one hand and the pigeon under his other arm.)

HAO: Stop it now! Where have you learned such unruly manners?

TING *(still running from Yuan Yuan):* Grandfather, she she . . .

YUAN *(shouts laughingly):* You can't get away. You can't get away! Just where do you think you can hide?

(As Zeng Ting approaches where Zeng Hao is sitting, and ducks behind his sofa, Yuan Yuan throws the lighted firecrackers at them. Zeng Ting and Zeng Hao both scream in fear, amid the "pic-paaa" noise of the firecrackers. While Yuan Yuan roars at her own mischief, Xiao Zhuer is rolling with laughter by the living room door.)

HAO: What's gotten into you, you little devil?

YUAN: Grandpa Zeng!

HAO: What's all this ruckus about?

YUAN *(coyly):* Look, Grandpa Zeng *(stretches her neck and shows him her wetted hair, and points at Zeng Ting.)* He threw water on me first!

VOICE OF A MAN *(from outside, laughing):* Where are you, my little monkey?

YUAN *(mischievously):* I'm in here, Old Ape! *(Laughing and skipping, exits through the living room door.)*

HAO *(to Siyi):* See that? Now how can we set up Sufang with

such an uncouth family? *(Turns to Zeng Ting):* Did you throw
water on her?

TING *(timidly):* She, she dared me.

HAO: Get down on your knees!

SIYI: Grandfather . . . I think . . .

HAO: Get down on your knees!

(Knowing that there is no way out, Zeng Ting kneels down.)

HAO: May as well let the Yuans see how we discipline our children here in the Zeng family.

*Yuan Yuan enters happily, hand in hand, with her "Old Ape," the
anthropologist Yuan Rengan. The "Old Ape" isn't actually that old; he
looks about forty years of age. Yet the bald spot on top of his head is
prominent. The few remaining hairs are combed across his shiny bald
spot, suggesting that he had a full head of hair once upon a time. He
is not a tall man, but he stands very straight, and looks healthy and
well-fed. Wearing a pair of old yellow jodhpurs, muddy black riding
boots, and a brown shirt open at the collar, he looks like an automobile
mechanic. Yet his eyes are alert and full of humor, with a trace of
cynicism. They bear the contemplative expression often characteristic of
scholars.*

YUAN *(speaking as they walk into the room):* So, Father, Xiao Zhuer
comes along with this stick of incense; so I lit my firecracker
with it and started chasing him. I aimed right for his leg . . .

MR. YUAN *(nods smilingly as he listens):* Uh-huh . . . uh-huh . . .
oh. *(Sees that Zeng Hao is already standing to greet him.)* Old
Master Zeng. Thank you so much for inviting us today. Here
we are imposing on you again.

HAO: Oh it's just a little gathering to celebrate the festival. *(Zeng
Hao guides Mr. Yuan to the seat of honor.)* Please have a seat,
Mr. Yuan: Sit here.

YUAN *(seeing Zeng Ting kneeling on the floor, yells):* Look, Father,
look! He's kneeling on the floor.

HAO: Don't pay any attention to him. Please be seated!

MR. YUAN *(shocked as he looks at Zeng Ting):* What happened?

HAO: My grandson here was very naughty! He splashed a bucket of water on your daughter . . .

MR. YUAN *(smiles apologetically)* Oh my! Get up, get up! I'm the one who gave him that bucket of water . . .

HAO *(dumbfounded):* But, but . . . *(Not knowing how to end this matter, looks at Zeng Ting sternly.)* But he's still a bad boy.

MR. YUAN *(smiles):* Oh, there's nothing wrong with being a little mischievous, there's nothing wrong with that. Come on, get up now.

SIYI *(takes the opportunity to free her son):* Get up now, Ting, and thank Uncle Yuan!

TING *(gets on his feet):* Thank you Uncle Yuan.

MR. YUAN *(to Zeng Ting):* I'm sorry about this. Next time you should throw water on me.

HAO *(cannot bear to listen to all this any longer):* Mr. Yuan, please have a seat. Ruizhen, pour the wine. *(Heads toward the dinner table.)*

MR. YUAN *(still smiling):* My little friend, you should never kneel alone. When you kneel, you know, you're much shorter than everybody else, and that doesn't look good at all.

SIYI: Mr. Yuan, come sit here.

MR. YUAN: Oh yes, time to eat. I'm going to make myself at home. Yuan-er.[26]

(Zhang Shun carries in a plate of hot food, sets it on the table, and exits.)

SIYI: Come over here, Miss Yuan, and sit next to your father.

(After the two are seated, the rest of the family take their places.)

HAO *(raises wine glass):* Today is Midautumn Festival and my son Wenqing is leaving home. Since he has seldom had the chance to enjoy your good company, Mr. Yuan, we're happy to take this opportunity to get together. Come, come let's drink to you.

---

[26]Chinese parents commonly add the suffix "-er" (literally, "child") to given names of their children as a sign of affection and intimacy.

MR. YUAN: Thank you, thank you. *(Downs the whole glass of wine.)*
I hear that Mr. Zeng is a real connoisseur of tea . . .

(Noise of quarreling can be heard from the outside.)

HAO: Ruizhen, why don't you go out and see who's making all that noise?

YUAN *(to Ruizhen):* I'll go for you.

(Siyi whispers something to Wenqing. Wenqing gets up, picks up the wine decanter, and walks over to Zeng Hao, with Siyi following him. Yuan Yuan puts down her chopsticks and runs out through the living room door.)

SIYI *(wine glass in hand):* Your daughter-in-law would like to make a toast to you, Father.

HAO *(still sitting):* Oh, there's no need for that . . . really . . .

SIYI *(respectfully):* Wenqing wants to say goodbye to you, Father.

WENQING *(softly):* Father, this is to bid you farewell.

(Wenqing kneels and kowtows three times. Ruizhen and Ting both stand up. Mr. Yuan looks on wide-eyed with curiosity. At the same time, a clamor of angry voices can be heard.)

VOICE OF COLLECTOR A: Are you going to pay or not?!

VOICE OF COLLECTOR B *(almost simultaneously):* This is Midautumn Festival, and we've been waiting all morning!

VOICE OF COLLECTOR C *(almost simultaneously):* Pay up this time and your credit's good. But if you don't give us any money, how can we give you any credit? You're really . . .

HAO: What's going on?

SIYI: Must be people quarreling next door.

HAO *(relieved, to Yuan Yuan):*[27] Help yourself. *(To Zeng Ting and*

---

[27]No stage directions are given for Yuan Yuan's reentry. Earlier editions of the play show that Zeng Hao is addressing Yuan Rengan, *not* Yuan Yuan. This is at a point in the script which has been heavily revised. In the earlier editions, Yuan Yuan does not reenter until the collectors barge in on the Zengs. She also serves as a cheerleader while her father and the "Peking Man"—a worker whose physique is being studied for its resemblance to the prehistoric Peking Man by Yuan Rengan—scatter the money collectors. The deletion of this scene from the present version changes the conclusion of act 1. In the earlier editions, the "Peking Man" and Yuan Rengan successfully drove out the money collectors after a fist fight. In this revised edition, without the "Peking Man," the collectors close in on Zeng Hao as the curtain closes.

Ruizhen, kindly): You two should also say goodbye to your
father.

*(Ruizhen and Zeng Ting then get up together and walk over to Wen-
qing's place with the wine decanter. Zeng Ting pours wine for Wenqing.)*

SIYI *(instructing them skillfully):* Now say, "We wish you a safe
journey, Father."

RUIZHEN AND TING *(in unison, mechanically):* We wish you a safe
journey, Father.

SIYI: Now say, "Please write to us often, Father."

RUIZHEN AND TING *(mechanically):* Please write to us often, Father.

SIYI *(still instructing):* Now say, "Your son and daughter-in-law
can no longer serve you."

RUIZHEN AND TING *(mechanically):* Your son and daughter-in-law
can no longer serve you. *(They make a move to return to their
seats.)*

SIYI *(hastily):* Kowtow, you silly kids! *(Looks at Mr. Yuan, proudly.)*

*(Ruizhen and Zeng Ting kowtow, bowing three times. Wenqing stands
up. As the solemn kowtow goes on, more cursing and quarreling can
be heard.)*

VOICE OF COLLECTOR A: How can you people even celebrate this
festival?

COLLECTOR B *(almost simultaneously):* You still owe us money from
the Dragon Festival last May. And now you won't even give
us a cent.

COLLECTOR C *(almost simultaneously):* It's less than five hundred
dollars. Why such a problem?

VOICE OF ZHANG SHUN *(trying to persuade them):* Don't stand
around here screaming and yelling like that. Get out of here!
Get going! The Old Master is here . . .

COLLECTOR A *(sarcastically):* So what if he's here! What does he
think he is, some kind of rich man?

COLLECTOR B *(almost simultaneously):* He's no different from us if
he can't pay his bills.

COLLECTOR C *(almost simultaneously)*: Bunch of bankrupt has-
  beens!

*(The quarreling continues. Mr. Yuan turns his head and listens atten-
tively.)*

HAO: What's really going on out there?

SIYI: Could be the people next door . . .

*(Sufang hurries in through the living room door amid the sound of
quarreling.)*

HAO: Who is that?

SUFANG *(concealing the truth)*: Oh, nobody.

SIYI *(smiles slyly)*: Mr. Yuan. Let me introduce you. This is Miss
  Su. *(Yuan Rengan gets up. Siyi turns to Sufang.)* This is Mr.
  Yuan!

*(Chen Naima, wearing an old apron, enters hurriedly through the living
room door with a big plate of food. Xiao Zhuer follows her, holding his
grandmother's skirt with one hand and carrying the pigeon in the other.)*

CHEN *(saying as she walks, in an annoyed tone)*: Let go of me, Xiao
  Zhuer. Don't be such a pest! *(Sets the plate down on the table
  and shakes her hands.)* Oooh! it's hot!

SUFANG *(in a low voice)*: Cousin Siyi!

SIYI *(raises her chopsticks)*: Mr. Yuan, this dish is Miss Su's . . .
  (Sufang tugs on Siyi's sleeve.)

SIYI *(turns to Sufang)*: Huh?

HAO *(raises chopsticks)*: Please, help yourself. Help yourself!

SUFANG *(simultaneously, in a worried tone)*: The man from the coffin
  shop, he . . . they . . .

SIYI *(without paying attention to her, rolls her eyes and says merrily)*:
  Please don't stand on ceremony. *(To Mr. Yuan)*: Our Miss
  Su *(pointing to Sufang)* went to a lot of trouble to make this
  dish especially for you! *(Unconsciously looks and smiles at
  Wenqing.)*

HAO *(raises his chopsticks again)*: Please have some more.

*(The living room door is thrown open and all the collectors barge in
with Zhang Shun in the middle, unable to block their entry.)*

ZHANG SHUN: Stop, stop. We have guests inside.

COLLECTOR A *(pushes him aside):* You keep out of this! Give us our money, we're not asking for your lives. Old Master, Da Nainai *(extending his hand),* if you have the money, pay up. Don't you think it's about time?
(They slowly approach Zeng Hao.)

Curtain

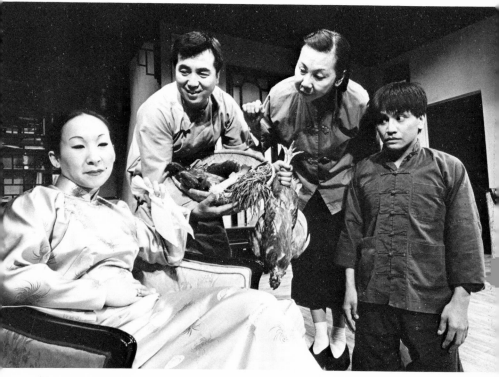

(*Zeng Siyi, Zhang Shun, Chen Naima, Xiao Zhuer*)

CHEN: . . . there's really nothing fancy to bring you from the country. I've just picked some leeks, celery, kohlrabi, cucumbers . . . and there's a little millet, some eggs, and a couple of old hens. [Act 1]

(*Zeng Ruizhen, Zeng Wenqing, Zeng Ting, Zeng Siyi, Zeng Hao, Yuan Rengan, Yuan Yuan*)

RUIZHEN AND TING: We wish you a safe journey, Father. . . . Please write to us often, Father. [Act 1]

(*Zeng Wenqing, shadow of Peking Man*)

VOICE OF MR. YUAN: You see, this is the original Peking Man. People in those days loved when they wanted to, hated when they wanted to. . . . There was no man-eating moral code or civilization as we have today. And yet they lived very happy lives. [Act 2]

(*Sufang, Zeng Ruizhen, Zeng Ting, Yuan Yuan*)
YUAN: Oh, only seventeen and you're going to be a father. . . . Oh, a
little father, a seventeen-year-old father. [Act 2]

(Sufang, Ruizhen)

RUIZHEN: No, Auntie Su, I can't wait any longer. I have to leave this
place, I've already waited two years. [Act 2]

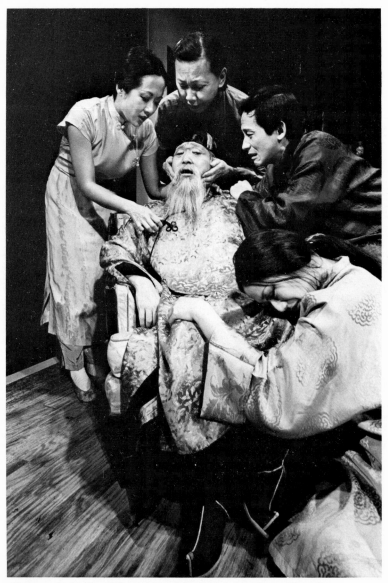

(Sufang, Zeng Hao, Chen Naima, Zeng Wenqing, Zeng Wencai)
WENQING: Oh Father! Oh Father! It's all my fault! It's all my fault! [Act 2]

(*Zeng Ruizhen, Sufang*)

SUFANG: But Ruizhen, suddenly I feel so happy! My heart is so warm! It feels as if spring is here! Isn't this what life is all about? Just days and days full of sadness and happiness. [Act 3, scene 1]

(*Chen Naima, Zeng Wencai, Jiang Tai, Policeman, Zeng Ting*)
JIANG: Here, this is my family! And this is my wife! And this is my
father-in-law, Mr. Zeng Hao! [Act 3, scene 2]

Act 2

*Around 11 o'clock the same evening, in the parlor of the Zeng house.
In the distance, a lonely blind fortune-teller bangs his cymbals intermittently in a desolate lane, making his way home. The Zeng house is
surrounded by a deathly silence. Occasionally the sounds of women and
children's voices can be heard. These are the sad, slow calls of peddlers
coming from the bleak streets in the distance.*

*In the room, the gauze-shaded lamp casts a dim circle of light. The
scrolls and art objects are only faintly visible in the darkness. The bamboo painting on the wall appears particularly obscure. All the curtains
are tightly drawn. A streak of light coming through a tear in the gauze
lamp shade falls on the door leading to the main living room. All the
white papered partitions are shut. Except for the wooden carvings on
the extreme lower edge of the partitions, the doors all appear as huge
snow-white paper screens. Threads of light seep through the cracks between the partitions, as human shadows play about on their surfaces.
Occasionally, the silence is broken by coughs and faint conversations in
the main living room.*

*Several candleholders stand on the long, narrow table along the left
wall, and in one of these holders is a half-burned candle. A low table
stands in the middle of the room. On it is a tiny red clay stove holding
a small iron kettle. The room looks unusually clean and tidy. A fire is
burning merrily, flickering out of the lower opening of the stove. The
water in the kettle is making a moaning noise, as if there were a child
trapped inside, crying sadly. To one side is an elegant redwood table
holding a small, exquisite tea set. Wenqing is sitting on a low stool next
to the burner, which illuminates his pale face, lost in thought. Chen
Naima is sitting on a small sofa which has been moved in from the other*

side of the room. She is trimming Xiao Zhuer's fingernails with a pair
of scissors. The boy is dozing on a small stool.

In the study there is a single dim light. A sleepy-eyed Zeng Ting
is seen, softly reciting [the prose-poem] "Autumn Sounds." From a
distance, the clapping sounds of the night watchman can be heard com-
ing from the end of a long lane.

CHEN *(trimming Xiao Zhuer's nails and chatting):* Really, Master
    Wenqing, are you still thinking of leaving tomorrow?
(Wenqing nods.)
CHEN: I think you should forget it. Since you missed the train,
    you might as well stay another two or three days and see
    how it works out between Mr. Yuan and Miss Su.
(Wenqing shakes his head.)
CHEN: Do you think Mr. Yuan knew what was going on?
WENQING *(lowers his head and answers reluctantly):* I didn't pay any
    attention.
CHEN *(grinning):* I could tell that Mr. Yuan knew what was going
    on. He was looking in Miss Su's direction all during lunch.
(Wenqing stares at Naima as if he does not understand her.)
CHEN: Young Master, you think this whole thing . . .
(Wenqing cannot withhold a long sigh. Naima glances at Wenqing with-
out continuing what she wanted to say. Xiao Zhuer stirs in his sleep,
yawns, mumbles something incomprehensible, and dozes off again.)
CHEN *(clipping Xiao Zhuer's nails):* Ai! I think we should go home.
    (Points at Xiao Zhuer.) His mother's expecting us home to-
    night. *(Xiao Zhuer starts again, as Naima tries to support him*
    with her hands.) Don't move, my precious! Or else Grand-
    mother will cut you! *(Lovingly):* Ai, this boy must be very
    tired. He walked here all morning, then he played with Miss
    Yuan all day long. Country children aren't like city children:
    they eat when they are hungry, and sleep when they're
    tired. He's not like . . . *(glances over to Zeng Ting, who is*
    studying in the study, and says tenderly, softly): Master Ting,
    Master Ting!

TING *(reciting in a low voice):* "Alas! Plants and trees have no emotion, at a given time they wither and fall; man too is a living creature, the most blessed and gifted of all. Countless thoughts vex his mind, a myriad of activities wear on his body. What moves him within in turn disturbs the essence of his being. Man's thoughts reach far beyond his powers of attainment; his worries are such that his wisdom is of no avail. . . ."

WENQING: Let him study, his grandfather is going to quiz him on that soon.

(The night watchman's drum can be heard from the alley.)

CHEN: He's up so late studying! It's Midautumn Festival! Ai, is that the third watch already?

WENQING: Yes, it's already the third watch.

CHEN: By this time, children in the village are all fast asleep. *(Finishes clipping the last finger of Xiao Zhuer.)* All right, get up and go to bed. Don't try to stay up like this.

XIAO *(rubs his eyes):* I don't, I don't want to go to sleep.

WENQING *(smiles):* But it's late, it's almost eleven o'clock.

XIAO *(musters his energies):* But I'm not tired.

CHEN *(a bit annoyed but still very lovingly):* All right, in that case you stay up all night. *(To Wenqing):* Really, these country bumpkins find everything in the city so fascinating. Look at him, he's so curious that he can't sleep.

(Xiao Zhuer takes a piece of peanut candy out of his pocket and puts it into his mouth, and then without thinking picks up and stares at his toy, the "gua da zui," which has been lying next to him.)

CHEN: Ai, on the very night of Midautumn Festival, we can't even see the moon . . . What's the matter? Why is Da Nainai staying inside? *(Calls):* Da Nainai! *(To Wenqing):* What's she doing in the bedroom? *(Gets up.)* Da Nainai! Da Nainai!

WENQING: Don't, don't bother her.

CHEN: Master Wenqing, then, then you'd better go in.

WENQING *(shakes his head and begins to mournfully recite "Coiffeured*

Phoenix" by Lu Yu)[1] ". . . The eastern wind blows cruelly and scatters my joy. Once bound by melancholy, there follow years of desolation—I am torn, I am torn, I am torn!"

CHEN *(sighs):* Ai, Young Master, you are an innocent victim of fate! You must have been indebted to Da Nainai in some previous life, so now she's come back to take you to account. What, what's really going on? She hasn't said a word all evening . . . what does she want?

WENQING: Who knows? She said her stomach was bothering her, and she felt nauseous.

CHEN *(turns and sees that Xiao Zhuer is beginning to get fidgety; scolds him as he starts playing with the teapot sitting on the low table):* Xiao Zhuer, put that down! Do you want a spanking?

(Xiao Zhuer puts the teapot down obediently.)

CHEN *(turns to Wenqing):* Isn't it strange? Wasn't Gu Laoye making a big fuss about moving out of here tonight? How come he's . . .

WENQING *(sighs):* He's just a lot of talk. *(Suddenly shows resentment in his voice.)* In a sense he's like me. I don't say much, and I don't get anything done. He rants and raves all day long, but he hasn't accomplished anything in his life either.

(Wencai enters through the study door, holding in her hands an unlit candle, a pair of chopsticks, and a plate of cured meat, preserves, and an assortment of dried nuts, which she has bought from the Dao Xiang Cun Restaurant.)

WENCAI *(tiredly):* Naima, you're still up!

CHEN: Oh, yes. How come Gu Laoye is drinking again?

WENCAI *(hiding her embarrassment):* Oh no, it's not him, it's me.

WENQING: You? . . . Ai, don't let him drink anymore.

WENCAI *(sighs and puts the chopsticks and the plate down):* Brother, he was crying to me again tonight.

CHEN: You mean Gu Laoye?

WENCAI *(with tears in her eyes, draws her handkerchief):* He says that

[1]"Chai Tou Feng." Lu Yu (1122–1210) was a prominent poet of the Sung dynasty.

he has let me down, and that he feels sorry about it. He says that life has passed him by. When I see him like that, I feel that I've been such a burden to him. Ai, it must be my awful fate that got him implicated in that embezzlement and made him lose his job. *(Tears run down her cheeks.)* Naima, where are the matches?

CHEN: I'll look . . .

WENQING *(picks up a box of matches from the low red table)*: Here they are!

(Naima takes the box from him and lights the candle for Wencai.)

WENCAI *(picks up a copper candlestick from the table)*: He said he was depressed and wanted a drink. You know, brother, he's so unhappy, I . . .

WENQING *(lets out a deep, long sigh)*: Let him drink then, maybe it will do him some good.

CHEN *(hands the lighted candle to Wencai)*: Is the Old Master still turning the lights off at eleven o'clock?

WENCAI *(puts the candle into the candlestick)*: Yes. *(Thoughtfully)*: That's why I am getting this candle ready. If the lights go out while he's drinking, he'll get upset again for sure.

CHEN: Let me help you carry that.

WENCAI: I can manage. *(Picks up the chopsticks, the plate, and the lighted candle, and enters her bedroom.)*

CHEN *(shakes her head)*: Ai, it's so hard being a woman.

(Wencai, having left the things in the bedroom, reenters hastily.)

WENCAI: Where's Jiang Tai?

CHEN: He just went into the living room.

WENQING: I suppose he's chatting with Mr. Yuan.

WENCAI *(has already walked over to the stove)*: Brother, do you still want this water?

WENQING *(shakes his head; tiredly)*: Wencai, you have to take care of yourself, don't strain yourself.

WENCAI *(forcing a smile, sorrowfully)*: No, I won't. *(Takes the kettle and exits through her bedroom door.)*

(Wenqing takes an Yi Xing kettle,[2] puts it on the stove, and then fans the flame lazily.)

TING *(picks up the book that he has been reading and stands up):* Father, I'm going over to Grandfather's room.

WENQING *(still attending to his earthern kettle, with his head lowered):* All right, go ahead.

CHEN *(walks up to Zeng Ting):* Master Ting! *(In a low voice):* If your grandfather asks you, don't tell him that your father is still here.

XIAO *(has been sitting there quietly; suddenly turns his head and says cleverly):* Just tell him he caught an early train.

CHEN *(amused):* Who told you that?

XIAO *(squinting):* You told me yourself.

CHEN: Oh, this child! *(To Zeng Ting):* Go ahead, Master Ting. After you finish reciting for your grandfather, hurry along to bed. If the Old Master still wants you to do more, just tell him that Chen Naima told you that you had to go to sleep.

TING: All right. *(Walks toward the study.)*

WENQING: Ting!

TING: What's the matter, Father?

WENQING *(concerned):* What's been on your mind the last couple of days?

TING *(tries to avoid the question):* Nothing, Father. *(Quickly exits through the study door.)*

CHEN *(follows Zeng Ting's exit admiringly, and then unconsciously turns and points at Xiao Zhuer):* You should follow his example. He's only two years older than you, and the number of the books he's read is more than all the grains of rice you've stuffed your face with. As for you, you eat four big bowls of rice at every meal, and your belly's filled with . . .

XIAO *(suddenly):* Grandmother, listen, who's calling me?

---

[2]Yi Xing potteries, manufactured in Yi Xing County, Jiangsu Province, are known to be the best earthenware in China.

CHEN: Nonsense! You think I'm totally deaf just because I can't hear things so well.

XIAO: It's the truth. Listen Grandmother, isn't that Miss Yuan . . .

CHEN: Where?

XIAO: Listen.

CHEN *(listens attentively)*: Miss Yuan is helping her father draw pictures of apes.

XIAO *(teasing his grandmother intentionally)*: Really, listen! Isn't that Miss Yuan calling me: "Xiao Zhuer! Xiao Zhuer!" Listen: "Xiao Zhuer, come over and help me feed the pigeons!" *(Suddenly grins broadly and mischievously.)* It's the truth, Grandmother, she's calling me to help her feed the pigeons. *(Slips away and starts running toward the living room.)*

CHEN *(chases after him, laughing)*: You tricky little monkey, you think you can fool your grandmother?

(Xiao Zhuer, laughing and running, gets to the sliding door of the living room, which looks like a huge screen. All of a sudden, the house is in complete darkness as, according to habit, all the lights in the Zeng residence are turned off at eleven o'clock. Almost simultaneously, a large crouching apelike shadow jumps onto the snowy white screen of the sliding door.)

XIAO *(sees the shadow and screams in fear)*: Grandmother! *(Runs back to Chen Naima and throws himself into her arms.)*

CHEN: Oh! What's that?

WENQING *(gets up; to Chen Naima)*: Light a candle!

CHEN: All right. *(Goes to light the candle.)*

VOICE OF YUAN RENGAN *(in the living room)*: You see, this is the original Peking Man. People in those days loved when they wanted to, hated when they wanted to. They cried when they were sad and they shouted when they were angry. They lived freely, without the restraints of morality, without the trappings of civilization. There was no pretension, no fraud, no deceit, no slander. The sun shone, the wind blew, and the rain fell. There was no man-eating moral code or

civilization as we have today. And yet they lived very happy
lives.

*(Suddenly one section of the folding door is opened, as the glow of the
gas light in the living room shines into the parlor. Jiang Tai is holding
the stub of a lit candle as he makes his entrance with Yuan Rengan.
Jiang Tai is wearing a Western-style vest, while Yuan Rengan still has
his brown shirt on, with sleeves rolled up. He has a pipe in his mouth
out of which smoke is curling.)*

JIANG *(a bit intoxicated, responds to the last sentence very agreeably):*
And yet they lived very happy lives.

VOICE OF YUAN YUAN *(in the living room):* Xiao Zhuer, come over
here!

XIAO: Yes! *(Runs into the living room.)*

JIANG *(still savoring the meaning of Mr. Yuan's comment, sets down
the candle excitedly, and repeats as if to himself):* And yet they
lived very happily. Right you are, Mr. Yuan, it's so true! You
couldn't be more correct! Look at how we live! Either we
walk around depressed all day or we never stop complaining. Or it's that endless worrying about death, or about life,
or about our lack of accomplishments, or about not having
the right spiritual attitude, or about not having enough to
eat, or not having the right coffin to die in. Day in and day
out we hope and hope. And yet there isn't any real hope.
For instance *(points at Wenqing),* he . . .

WENQING: Stop grumbling, or else Mr. Yuan'll think you foolish.

JIANG *(positively):* No, no, Mr. Yuan is an anthropologist, he
won't make fun of the weaknesses of the human race! Sit
down for awhile, Mr. Yuan, let's talk. *(Sits around the stove
with Mr. Yuan and picks up a cigarette from the redwood table;
says suddenly):* Now, where was I?

MR. YUAN *(smiles):* You said *(points at Wenqing),* take him, for
instance!

JIANG: Oh, take him, for instance. Oh *(to Wenqing, miserably),* I
really don't want to go on complaining, but if you won't let
me say a few things, then I, what else can I do? What else

can I live for? *(To Yuan Rengan):* All right, take him, for example, this brother-in-law of mine. He's a good man, one-hundred-and-twenty-percent good! But I know he is suffering greatly inside.

WENQING: Don't talk nonsense!

JIANG *(smiles shrewdly):* Oh, you can't hide it from me, I'm not *that* stupid. *(Pointing at Wenqing, to Yuan Rengan, in a straight-forward tone):* He suffers because he wants a happy family and he wants to spend the rest of his life with a woman who truly understands him. *(Excitedly):* Of course, his desire is only natural and reasonable, and he deserves our sympathy. And would you believe, many years ago he found a woman who understood him. But he didn't have the courage to go after her; when he finally did meet her, he was too scared to make her his own, so he let her grow up from a child to a young woman, and from a young woman to an old maid; he let her wither and die like a flower. And the whole time he stood by suffering. And she suffered too; to this very day, this woman is still . . .

WENQING *(impatiently):* You're really drunk!

JIANG *(laughs and waves his hand):* Don't worry, I'm not drunk. I promise you I'll stop right here and say no more. *(To Yuan Rengan):* You know, letting that woman rot away in a family like this—like a coffin rotting in an old graveyard, decaying slowly—so that all she can do is sigh and dream, sitting around waiting and suffering all day long, getting lazier and lazier, to the point that she can't even move anymore. She's too scared to love, too scared to hate, too scared to cry, even too scared to scream. Now *that* is degeneration, human degeneration. Now *(points at himself)*, take me, for example . . . *(strikes a match and lights his cigarette, puffing away as he speaks).* After studying for more than twenty years . . .

MR. YUAN *(smiles with his pipe in his mouth):* I knew you'd finally get to this.

JIANG *(talks endlessly and fluently):* Naturally. I won't just criticize others and say nothing about myself. Take me, for instance, I love money, I want money, and I never stop thinking about how I can get my hands on a large sum of money so I can give it to my friends and all the poor people to spend. I want to follow what Du Fu[3] said in a poem and build numerous elegant mansions for all my poor friends so that they can eat, drink, and live for free. They can do scientific research, study the arts and literature, or do whatever they want to do, for the benefit of China and all mankind. And yet, Mr. Yuan, I'm an unlucky man. No matter where I go I'm always rejected. I've never had a lucky break. For some strange reason, whenever I start a new career, the whole thing falls apart. When we plan our lives, our heads are always in the clouds; but when we live our lives, we always have to compromise. All we can do is sigh, fantasize, and feel miserable. We live only to deprive worthy people of their daily bread. We are the living dead, the ghosts, the dying! Just like you said (*pointing at his own chest*), it's people like us who are really (*pointing at the huge shadow of "Peking Man"*) his prodigal sons!

MR. YUAN (*has been listening to him, silently nodding in good humor all along; picks up a teacup, smiling*): Have some tea!

JIANG (*takes the teacup from him*): Right, now take tea-drinking, for instance. This brother-in-law of mine is a true connoisseur of tea. Before he drinks he must first wash his hands, rinse his mouth, burn incense, and sit quietly in meditation. The tip of his tongue can determine the character of the leaves, their age, their origin, and the manner in which they were processed. He can also tell us whether the water is from a mountain, a stream, a well, or melted from snow; and he can tell if the water was boiled on a charcoal fire or with coal or wood. We drink tea when we're thirsty; but

---

[3]Du Fu (712–770), one of the most prominent poets in Chinese history, lived and wrote during the Tang dynasty.

once it enters his mouth, it takes on endless implications that run the gamut from vulgarity to refinement. Yet, what's the use of all that? He can't grow tea, he can't sell tea, he can't even export tea. All he can do is *drink tea*. No matter how refined and how good he is at it, it's still merely drinking tea. So what's the use? Tell me, what's the use?

(Wencai enters from her bedroom.)

WENCAI: Tai!

JIANG: I'll be right there!

CHEN *(walks over and taps him)*: Hurry up, Gu Laoye!

JIANG *(stands up, but still reluctant to leave)*: Take me, for instance . . .

CHEN: Enough of this endless "take me for instance," "take me for instance." Mr. Yuan must be tired of your chattering.

JIANG: I say, Dr. Yuan, you don't mind my saying a little more, do you?

MR. YUAN *(smiles)*: Oh, of course not, please go ahead!

JIANG: So, for instance . . . *(Wencai comes over and tries to persuade him to go back to their bedroom; he says to Wencai almost in a pleading tone)*: Wencai, let me continue, just let me say a little more! *(To Yuan Rengan)*: Take me, for instance, I love good food, I know how to eat, and I can take you to all the best restaurants in town. *(Gets a bit conceited and starts quickly running down his endless list of favorite restaurants and their specialities.)* For instance, there's the mutton firepot at the Noonday Towers, roast duck at the Economy Foodshop, baked rolls at the Harmony House, mullet caviar at the Sunrise Restaurant, and stewed duck at the Temple of Perfection. As for snacks, there's minced pork noodles at the Cozy Kitchen, fried dough drops at Mu's Ranch House, sizzling tripe soup at the House of Jin, fried dumplings at the Capital Restaurant, not to mention . . .

WENCAI: Let's go!

JIANG: . . . not to mention spiced lamb at the Full Moon House, pickled vegetables at Six Times Around, fermented bean curd at Wang's Restaurant, sour plum soup at The Distant Memory, multicolored pudding at Triple Serendipity House, stuffed rolls at the Generosity House, sliced pork at the Crockpot Place, rice wine at Apricot Blossoms in Spring. All the managers there are my buddies. In all these places there isn't a single chef, a single waiter, a single cashier who doesn't know me. And yet what's the use? I can't cook and I can't run a restaurant; I'd never be able to open up a big Li Hongzhang chop-suey house abroad and earn foreigners' money. All I can do is *eat! (Unintentionally talks of his own weaknesses; as if pinching his own nerves, starts pounding on his chest.)* Whatever I do, I fail at! We went into the red when I worked for the government, I owed money when I went into business, and my whole education's been useless! *(Painfully):* I just hang around my father-in-law's place all day long, talking, complaining, criticizing, and yelling at people. I can't even control myself anymore; all I can do is say things no one wants to hear!

WENCAI *(interrupting):* Tai!

JIANG *(sobbing):* All day long I show people how unhappy and useless I am. They call me a good-for-nothing behind my back. Oh, Wencai, I'm such a good-for-nothing, deep down I know I've let you down! *(Suddenly bursts into tears.)* I'm such a burden to you!

WENCAI *(cries continuously):* Tai, Tai! Don't be so upset, it's me who's no good, it's me who's been a burden.

CHEN: Let's take him inside, he's had too much to drink again.

JIANG *(shakes his head):* I haven't, I haven't, I just feel so miserable, I feel so miserable.

(Jiang Tai, supported by Chen Naima and Wencai, exits into the bedroom.)

WENQING *(sighs):* Have some tea.

MR. YUAN: I've already had a lot of water today, and I ate so much at lunch. Mr. Zeng, I want to ask you to do me a favor . . .

WENQING: Yes . . .

MR. YUAN: I . . .

(Sufang enters through the study door, with a blanket in one hand and a candle in the other.)

MR. YUAN: Miss Su.

(Sufang nods at him.)

WENQING: Is Father asleep?

(Sufang shakes her head.)

WENQING: Mr. Yuan, you were saying?

(Jiang Tai reemerges from his bedroom, holding a half-empty bottle of brandy.)

JIANG *(smiling):* Would you like to come in and have a couple of drinks, Mr. Yuan?

MR. YUAN: No thanks *(points at the huge shadow):* he's still waiting for me!

JIANG *(raises the bottle):* Good brandy, Wenqing, you . . .

(Wenqing does not reply, but glances over at Sufang.)

JIANG *(puzzled):* Oh, why are the three of you . . .

VOICE OF NAIMA *(from his bedroom):* Gu Laoye!

JIANG *(shakes his head and sighs):* Ai, no one pays any attention to me, no one pays any attention to me. *(Exits into his bedroom.)*

WENQING: Mr. Yuan, you were saying . . .

VOICE OF YUAN YUAN *(from the living room):* Father, Father! Come over and look, I've finished the Peking Man's silhouette.

MR. YUAN *(glances at Sufang and Wenqing):* Tell you later. *(Then, humorously and knowingly):* It's nothing important. My Little Monkey is calling me.

(Yuan Rengan opens one section of the screen-like folding door and exits. The glow from the living room escapes briefly into the parlor, until the door is closed again. The huge shadow of the "Peking Man" stands out on the white screen. Silence; and the distant gong of the night watchman can be heard.)

WENQING *(expectantly):* Did Naima give you the note?

(Sufang nods in silence.)

WENQING *(in a low voice):* I, I wanted to see you once more before I left.

(Sufang unconsciously glances at the door of Wenqing's bedroom.)

WENQING *(points at the door):* She closes the door when she sleeps. *(Lowers his head.)*

(Sufang sits down.)

WENQING *(suddenly):* Sufang!

(Sufang gets up again.)

WENQING: What is it?

SUFANG: Uncle asked me to bring him the medical books.

(Chen Naima enters from Wencai's bedroom.)

CHEN: Oh, you're here, Miss Su. *(Instantly walks toward the study door.)*

WENQING: Where're you going, Naima?

CHEN *(finds an excuse):* I want to see if Master Ting has finished his homework. *(Exits through the study door.)*

(From the distance comes the mournful gong of the night watchman.)

WENQING: Sufang, I'm definitely leaving tomorrow, I don't think *(pause)* I'll ever come back to this house.

SUFANG *(affirmatively):* It's only right that you never come back again.

WENQING: Yes, I've decided never to come back. I've been think- ing about it all night, and I really feel that it's me, that I'm the cause of your wasting the last ten years of your life. I've hurt you and I've hurt myself; and it's all because I always thought, I've always thought that maybe one day, we could . . . *(sees Sufang frown and rub her forehead).* Sufang, are you all right?

SUFANG *(tiredly):* I'm exhausted.

WENQING *(sorrowfully):* Poor Sufang, I don't even want to think about how you're going to live here from now on. You're like that pigeon, locked helplessly in a cage. Waiting, wait- ing, waiting, until some day . . .

SUFANG *(shakes her head):* No, don't say that!

WENQING *(sadly):* Why, why do we have to be separated from

each other and suffer so much? Why can't we have wings and fly away together? *(Shakes his head.)* Oh, I really can't bear it like this!

SUFANG *(despondently):* Isn't this enough? What would satisfy you then?

WENQING *(suddenly):* Sufang, come south with me! *(Then instantly becomes hesitant.)* Come with me!

SUFANG *(shakes her head sorrowfully):* Why must you bring that up again?

WENQING *(regretful, saddened, says slowly with his head lowered):* If not, then, you'll have to agree to what the family discussed this morning.

SUFANG *(startled):* But, but why?

WENQING *(looks at Sufang, painfully):* After I leave I know I won't come back for the rest of my life. Sufang, I want you to promise me something. No matter what, you can't go on living here. *(Earnestly):* Just think, besides the rats that've been chewing up our paintings, what's left in this house? *(Sufang stares at him sadly.)* What's on your mind? What are you waiting for? Don't just sit there, talk to me. *(Suddenly gathers enough courage to say boldly):* Sufang, you, you should get, get married, and get away from this prison as soon as you can. I think Mr. Yuan is a reliable person, you . . .

(Sufang gets up slowly.)

WENQING *(also rises, begging her):* What do you plan to do, tell me.

(Sufang walks toward the study.)

WENQING *(painfully):* You can't walk away without saying anything, you can at least say yes or no.

SUFANG *(turns around):* Wenqing! *(Hands a letter to him and then walks away slowly.)*

(Perturbed, Wenqing takes the letter in his hand. Chen Naima enters hurriedly through the study door.)

CHEN *(urgently):* The Old Master's coming, he's right behind me.

(Pushing Wenqing.) Go inside, go inside, or else there'll be trouble. Go inside . . .

WENQING: Naima, I . . .

(Still muttering something, Chen Naima pushes Wenqing into his bedroom. Sufang stands dully. Resting on a cane, Zeng Hao enters through the study door with an oil lamp in his hand. He is wearing a long quilted gown and a pair of slippers, and has a woolen scarf around his neck.)

HAO *(sees Sufang; anxiously):* I've been waiting for you for a long time. *(To Naima):* Who just went inside?

CHEN: It was Da Nainai.

HAO *(sees the red clay stove):* Why, who's been making tea here?

CHEN: It was Gu Laoye. He was here drinking tea with Mr. Yuan a while ago!

HAO *(smiles condescendingly):* Tsk! What do they know about tea drinking! *(Suddenly sees the huge shadow on the door.)* And what's that?

CHEN: It's the "Peking Man" that Mr. Yuan's been drawing.

HAO *(scornfully):* "Peking Man"? What nonsense!

CHEN: Old Master, you'd better go back and sleep.

HAO: No, I want to stay up for awhile. You go to bed now.

SUFANG: Naima, I've made your bed for you.

CHEN: Oh, thank you. *(Touched by Sufang's kindness.)* Oh, Miss Su, you . . . *(very pleased).* Yes, I'll go see *(Exits through the study door.)*

(Zeng Hao begins his nightly ritual inspection of the house.)

SUFANG *(following Zeng Hao around):* It's late, Uncle, you should go to sleep. Everything's all right.

HAO *(inspecting a corner of the parlor):* This house was passed down to us as the fruit of our ancestor's hard work, so we must take care to prevent fires. *(Suddenly):* What's that smoke and that glowing thing over there on the floor?

SUFANG: It's a cigarette butt.

HAO *(warily):* That's very dangerous. It must be Jiang Tai's. He's always been like that, he never puts out his cigarettes properly.

(Sufang picks up the cigarette butt, and is about to throw it into the stove.)

HAO: There's so much left and yet he still threw it away! How wasteful! *(Turns and sniffs.)* Sufang, do you smell something?

SUFANG: No.

HAO: Did anybody come to visit?

SUFANG: Nobody.

HAO *(sniffs):* That's strange, it smells like somebody's smoking opium.

SUFANG: It could be that you've smoked a little too much tobacco yourself today.

HAO: Oh, I'm getting old, even my own nose is failing me. *(Suddenly):* Did Wenqing really leave?

SUFANG: He's gone.

HAO: Don't lie to me.

SUFANG: He's really gone.

HAO: Ai, that's good. This son of mine alone has caused me so much anguish. After so many attempts he's finally stopped smoking opium, and now he's gone.

SUFANG: It's late, you should go to bed.

HAO *(sits on a sofa and starts complaining):* They lie to me all the time. Life's so meaningless once you get old. My children are all worthless. Not a single one of them is concerned about me. *(Tragically):* Not one of them cares for me, sympathizes with me, or really loves me. I slaved away for so many years, and now they're all just waiting for me to die.

SUFANG: Uncle, please don't feel that way.

HAO: But I know, I know. *(Bitterly):* My daughter-in-law's the worst of them all. All she thinks about is how she can get her hands on my money. I know she purposely lured that bunch of thugs in here this afternoon just to embarrass me. *(Grits his teeth.)* You know, she doesn't even want that coffin to stay in the house, her own father's coffin. Have you ever seen such an inconsiderate, unfilial, heartless woman? And she's supposed to come from a scholar's family; she's supposed to be . . .

(The pattering sound of a sudden downpour can be heard from outside; the leaves are stirred and reply, murmuring "sa sa.")

HAO: And she's even a parent herself . . .

SUFANG *(listens attentively by the small window of the study)*: Look Uncle, it's raining. Go to bed now. You've done enough talking tonight.

HAO *(shakes his head)*: No, I don't want to sleep. I'm old, and my children are unfilial. It's so awful to be all by myself in the middle of the night with no one to keep me company. *(Rubs his thighs painfully.)* Oh!

SUFANG: What's the matter?

HAO *(moans)*: Oh, it hurts, my legs really hurt!

(Gong of the night watchman outside.)

(Sufang brings over a low stool and rests Zeng Hao's legs on it. After covering his legs with a woolen blanket, she pulls another low stool over and sits next to him, pummeling his legs gently.)

SUFANG: Feel better?

HAO *(moans)*: Yes, yes. My feet are cold as ice. Sufang, have you filled my hot water bottle yet?

SUFANG: Yes.

HAO *(reminiscing)*: Your aunt was so good to me when she was alive. When it got a little chilly at night, she would immediately light the charcoal stove and warm some rice wine for me. And then she would always warm my bed long before . . . *(As if suddenly remembers something)*: My hot water bottle, where did you put it?

SUFANG *(still pummeling his legs)*: I already put it under your blanket. *(Yawns.)*

HAO *(very pleased)*: Oh, there isn't much that we old people wish for. First comes food, clothing, and warmth, then comes obedient and filial children. As you can see *(starts complaining again)*, none of mine are obedient. They're all filled with strange notions. Not one of them will listen to me and look out for their old father! *(Sees that Sufang has lowered her head.)* Sufang, do you want to go to sleep?

SUFANG *(startled as she is awakened from her doze):* Oh, no.

HAO *(sympathetically):* You must be exhausted. You hardly got a wink of sleep last night and you've been waiting on me all day today. No wonder you're so tired. Go to bed now. *(With resentment in his voice):* I know you're not listening to me anymore.

SUFANG *(rubs her eyes and yawns slightly):* No, Uncle, I'm not ready to go to sleep yet. I'm listening.

HAO *(cannot resist complaining again):* Who can blame you? They're all asleep already. I've been so unfortunate in my old age, not even my own flesh and blood spend any time with me, they think that I'm a burden . . .

SUFANG *(lowers her head):* No, Uncle, I don't feel that way, I've never . . .

HAO *(grumbles):* Sufang, don't try to fool me, I understand. Even if they haven't said anything to you, I know you can't bear this any longer. *(Moans.)* Oh, I feel so dizzy.

SUFANG: Nobody has said anything to me. I, I was just a little sleepy then.

HAO *(nagging):* You're still so young, and yet you spend so much of your time with an old man like me. I understand your frustration. *(Lets out a long sigh.)* Ai, what good does it do you to follow me around? I don't have money anymore, there's no happiness in the present and there's no hope for the future. *(Laments with a sigh.)* My future lies in that coffin, that coffin. I . . . *(pummels his own legs)* Oh!

SUFANG *(pummels harder as she tries to explain again):* It's true, uncle, I just had a tired spell a few minutes ago.

HAO *(tearfully, looks at Sufang):* You can't hide it from me, Sufang *(half accusing, half complaining)*, I know you hate me inside, you're not a child . . .

SUFANG: Uncle, I want to take care of you.

HAO (*waves his hand*): Sufang, you don't have to massage me anymore.

SUFANG: But I'm not tired.

HAO (*presses on her hand*): No, don't. I want to tell you something. (*Nagging.*) I don't want you to suffer like this for the rest of your life. I'm looking out for you. If you marry a reliable person, I'll have peace of mind even if there's no one to take care of me. (*Sufang withdraws her hand unconsciously.*) Then I'll know I did right by you and didn't let your mother down, I . . .

SUFANG: No, uncle. (*Gets up slowly*).

HAO: But . . . (*sardonically*) at your age, you're not really young anymore . . .

SUFANG (*lowers her head in agony*): Please, Uncle, please don't say any more. I have no intention of leaving you.

HAO (*mercilessly*): Let me go on. You're not young anymore, and the best a woman of your age can hope for is to marry a widower. That situation is fine if his first children are nice, but if by some chance they're bad, and you have no savings of your own, then life would be . . .

SUFANG (*unable to stand it any longer*): Uncle, I, I've never thought about . . .

HAO (*smiles bitterly*): But, it's better for you to marry a widower than to stay here for the rest of your life. I understand that.

SUFANG (*painfully*): I, I . . .

HAO (*carries on incessantly*): I understand. As a woman gets older it's hard for her to find the perfect match. She won't marry someone beneath her, and it's hard to find someone worthy of her. Once she reaches thirty (*gets crueler as he talks on, stressing his every phrase*), her parents are no longer alive to protect her. She's all alone, with no one to be close to, and then she finally gets old, and no one's there to take care of her, no children, no children or relatives. She gets older and older, as old as me . . .

SUFANG (*murmurs continuously with grief and fear in her eyes*): No, no. *(Suddenly bursts into tears and cries.)* Uncle, why are you talking like this too! I have no intention of leaving you!

HAO *(painfully)*: Oh, I'm only looking out for you, looking out for you!

SUFANG *(sobbing)*: Uncle, please don't worry about me. I've told you that I would never get married.

HAO *(lets out a long sigh)*: Don't cry Sufang, your uncle won't be around for very much longer.

A lonely blind fortune-teller passes through the long, spooky lane outside the house, tapping his copper cymbals.)

HAO: What's that?

SUFANG: It's the blind fortune-teller on his way home *(Dries her tears in silence.)*

HAO: Don't cry. I won't live that much longer. And even if I'm a bother to you, it won't be too many more years. I know Siyi and Jiang Tai can't wait for me to die, so that they can divide up my money. But Sufang, you're my only devoted child!

SUFANG: But you, you won't. *(Starts to weep silently.)* Why do you always have to think that way? I haven't offended you today in any way, have I?

HAO *(stroking Sufang's hand)*: No, you've been nice, you're a good girl. But they all think your uncle's a rich man *(Sufang again withdraws her hands slowly.)* All they see is money pasted all over my face. To them, my heart isn't filled with love and kindness for them, but only full of gold and silver. *(Coughs.)* They are all waiting for me to die. Ai, life when you're old is so meaningless. *(Rubs his forehead.)* Oh, my head hurts so much. *(Wants to get up.)*

SUFANG *(helps him up)*: Then go to bed.

HAO *(sits up, and starts searching his pocket)*: But there is no money left. It was all spent on your aunt's funeral, for the maintenance of her grave, repairing this house, and lacquering my coffin every year. *(Pulls out a red bankbook from his pocket.)* This is the bankbook that Siyi is so curious about. *(Hands it over to Sufang.)* See how much is left? Sufang, what a pity, there's hardly anything left for you after I'm gone *(stands up)* . . .

SUFANG *(painfully)*: Uncle, I've never even thought about your money!

(Ruizhen enters through the study door.)

RUIZHEN: Grandfather, your medicine is ready, I put it in your room.

HAO: Oh!

(Claps of the night watchman. Dogs bark in the dark alley.)

HAO: Let's go, then.

(Zeng Hao, with the help of Ruizhen and Sufang, is about to make his exit through the study door when Zeng Ting enters through the study door with a book [bound in traditional Chinese style—the pages of the book sewn together with thread].)

TING: Grandfather, I've finished copying. Do you still want to continue with your lecture?

HAO *(shakes his head)*: It's late. *(Turns to Ruizhen.)* Ruizhen isn't coming with us, so why don't the two of you go and get some sleep.

(Sufang helps Zeng Hao out through the study door. Ruizhen stares at the stove while Zeng Ting walks up to the huge shadow, looks at it momentarily, and starts pacing back and forth in the parlor.)

TING *(trying to find something to say)*: Is Mother still up?

RUIZHEN: I think she's asleep.

TING *(hesitantly)*: How come you're not in bed yet?

RUIZHEN: I just finished preparing Grandfather's medicine. *(Suddenly feels nauseous and sits down.)*

TING *(a bit anxiously)*: Why are you sitting here then?

RUIZHEN *(rubs her chest)*: Oh, no reason. *(Disappointedly)*: Do you want me to leave?

TING *(tries to tolerate the situation)*: No, no.

(The sound of falling rain, and the desolate voice of a peddler calling: "Noodle cakes!")

TING *(looking out the window)*: It's really coming down!

RUIZHEN: Oh, yes it is.

(In the long lane outside, the peddler again calls in his deep voice: "Noodle cakes!")

TING *(lonesomely):* The old man who sells noodle cakes is back again.

RUIZHEN *(looks up):* Are you hungry?

TING: No.

RUIZHEN *(stands up):* You, you don't want to go to sleep yet?

TING: No, I don't. If you are tired, why don't you go ahead?

RUIZHEN *(lowers her head):* All right. *(Slowly walks toward the study door.)*

TING: Why you . . . why are you crying?

RUIZHEN: I'm not crying.

TING *(suddenly in a sympathetic tone, but hesitantly, halting at intervals):* If you need money . . . Mother just gave me twenty dollars today . . . it's on the pillow in the room . . . go ahead and take it if you want.

RUIZHEN *(sighs in despair):* All right.

TING *(with sympathy on his face, but somewhat reluctantly):* If, if you don't want to go back to the room alone, you can stay here for awhile.

RUIZHEN: No, I'll go back now.

(Zeng Ting almost sneezes but manages to hold it back.)

RUIZHEN *(turns):* Are you dressed warmly enough?

TING: I'm not cold.

(Ruizhen starts for the study door again.)

TING *(suddenly remembers something):* Oh, Mother just said . . .

RUIZHEN: What did she say?

TING: Mother said she wanted you to massage her legs.

RUIZHEN: All right. *(Turns and walks toward Wenqing's bedroom.)*

TING *(suddenly stops her):* Wait, don't go yet.

RUIZHEN *(listlessly):* What's the matter?

TING *(trying to win her sympathy):* Do, do you hate this family?

RUIZHEN: Me?

TING *(pressing):* Yes, do you?

(Ruizhen lowers her head melancholically.)

TING *(disappointed; softly):* You'd better go.

RUIZHEN *(halfway to Wenqing's bedroom, suddenly turns her head; half-hopeful, half-worried):* I want to tell you something.

TING: What's that?

RUIZHEN *(shyly):* I, I haven't been feeling too well lately.

TING *(anxiously):* Why didn't you tell me earlier?

RUIZHEN: I . . . was a little scared.

TING *(directly):* Scared of what? Why aren't you feeling well?

RUIZHEN *(hesitantly):* I'm nauseated all the time. I think . . .

TING *(muddleheadedly):* Oh, then throw up. *(Calls out):* Mother!

RUIZHEN *(stops him immediately):* What are you doing?

TING: Mother has some special pills in her room, they'll make you feel better.

RUIZHEN *(resentfully):* You!

TING *(perturbed):* Why, tell me, what else is wrong?

RUIZHEN *(disappointed):* Nothing, I, I . . . *(walks toward the bedroom.)*

TING: Why are you crying again?

RUIZHEN *(halts):* I'm not crying. *(Suddenly turns and looks at Zeng Ting and says sorrowfully):* Ting, don't you realize that you're a grown man now? Ting, we are . . .

TING *(explains hastily):* We're friends. You told me that we should be friends. We didn't choose to marry each other. Your girlfriend's right, I'm not your slave, and you're not mine. We're no more than friends to each other. We should each have our own freedom to go our own ways. You, don't you think that's right?

RUIZHEN *(suddenly says firmly):* Yes, I do!

VOICE OF SIYI *(calling from bedroom on the right):* Ruizhen, Ruizhen!

TING: Mother wants you.

RUIZHEN *(startled momentarily; then turns to Zeng Ting):* In that case, I'll go.

TING: Hmm.

(Ruizhen exits into the bedroom on the right.)

TING (*seeing that Ruizhen has left, gathers up his courage, and calls through the crack of the folding door in a low voice*): Yuan Yuan! Yuan Yuan!

(*Ruizhen reenters from Siyi's bedroom.*)

TING (*a bit embarrassed*): How come you . . .

RUIZHEN: Mother wants me to go get Auntie Su. (*Exits through the study door.*)

TING (*hesitates a little, sighs; then*): Yuan Yuan! Yuan Yuan!

(*A section of the folding door is opened, and light leaks through from the living room as Yuan Yuan enters.*)

YUAN: Oh, it's you again?

TING: Yuan Meimei, did you read my letter?

YUAN (*muddleheadedly*): Yes, I did.

TING (*abruptly*): Did you read the poem I wrote for you, the one in the letter?

YUAN (*nods, and naively*): Yes I did!

TING (*happily*): You did?

YUAN (*nods*): Yes, and my father said your handwriting is much better than mine.

TING (*utterly surprised*): You let your father read it?

YUAN (*suddenly wises up*): Don't be embarrassed, it doesn't matter. Father said that you only wrote a couple of characters incorrectly; you're still much better than I am.

TING: Then, what about the poem . . .

YUAN (*nods*): I let Father read it.

TING (*more frightened*): You let him read it too?

YUAN: But I couldn't understand it.

TING: Then your father . . .

YUAN (*shakes her head*): He said your style is really old-fashioned (*apologetically*). He couldn't understand it either!

TING: What else did he say?

(*Ruizhen and Sufang enter through the study door. As they are walking out of the study, Ruizhen suddenly sees Zeng Ting and Yuan Yuan from the corner of her eye, halts abruptly, and stands in the study.*)

Sufang, with a knitted baby dress in her hand, also stands there silently.)

YUAN: He said . . . *(abruptly)* he told me not to play with you anymore. But don't pay any attention to him, we'll go out and fly the kite tomorrow.

TING *(softly)*: Why can't we play together?

YUAN *(casually)*: Auntie Su just had a talk with Father.

TING *(frightened)*: What about?

YUAN: She said that your wife's going to have a baby.

TING *(shocked)*: What?

YUAN: That you're about to become a father! *(Curiously)*: Is it really true?

TING *(in the clouds, confused)*: Who, me?

YUAN: As soon as Auntie Su left, my father told me I shouldn't play with you anymore.

TING *(still confused)*: Me, a father?

YUAN *(suddenly)*: I'm fifteen, how old are you?

TING *(dumbfounded)*: Seventeen.

YUAN: Oh, only seventeen and you're going to be a father. *(Claps her hands.)* Oh, a little father, a seventeen-year-old father!

(Zeng Ting suddenly bursts out crying.)

YUAN: Don't cry. If you don't stop crying I'll get angry.

(Zeng Ting still cries.)

YUAN: Don't cry, Zeng Ting. Look, I'll even give you my pigeon. *(Raises Solitude in front of him.)*

TING *(shakes his head)*: No, no, I just want to cry!

VOICE OF YUAN RENGAN: Yuan Yuan!

YUAN *(in a low voice)*: My father is calling me now, I'll see you tomorrow. We'll go kite-flying or fishing, all right?

VOICE OF YUAN RENGAN: Yuan! Yuan!

YUAN: I'm coming Father.

(Yuan Yuan opens the folding door, runs in, and closes the door hastily. Strong wind, rain, and the desolate voice of the noodle cake peddler can be heard from the long lane outside of the house. Zeng Ting throws

himself onto a sofa and starts sobbing again. Ruizhen slowly enters from the study, while Sufang still stands numbly in the doorway.)

RUIZHEN *(walks up to Zeng Ting, bends over, and taps him on the shoulder, and says in a pitying tone):* Don't cry now, Miss Yuan's gone.

TING *(raises his head):* Auntie, Auntie Su wasn't lying was she? *(Ruizhen looks at him and sighs.)*

TING *(weeps uncontrollably and in a bitter tone):* Oh, who was it that forced the two of us together! *(Gets up.)* Oh I could *(stamps his foot)* kill myself! *(Runs toward the study.)*

SUFANG: Ting!

(Zeng Ting does not turn to look; he dashes out the study door. Ruizhen falls on the stool clumsily.)

SUFANG *(walks over):* Ruizhen!

RUIZHEN: Auntie Su!

SUFANG *(strokes Ruizhen's hair):* Don't, don't you . . .

RUIZHEN *(suddenly wraps herself around Sufang):* I really want to die too!

SUFANG *(gently):* Ruizhen, my little sister.

RUIZHEN *(uncontrollably shedding tears and voicing her grievances):* Auntie Su, why did you have to tell Uncle Yuan about it? Why did you tell Miss Yuan not to have anything to do with him?

SUFANG *(sorrowfully):* Ruizhen, I love you too much, I can't bear to see you suffering like this any longer. *(Muddled and confused.)* I don't know why I went and told him about it. Like a fool, I just went to talk to Mr. Yuan. I can't even remember what I told him, and then I ran back out. Ruizhen, if from now on Ting could . . .

RUIZHEN *(painfully):* Don't be silly, Auntie Su, you know he doesn't like me. Can't you tell? He doesn't like me one bit!

SUFANG *(mournfully):* No, he's still a child. Someday he'll treat you better. Ai, Ruizhen, wait, wait patiently, someday this will all be over.

RUIZHEN *(stands up shaking her head, and says painfully and slowly):*

No, Auntie Su, I can't wait any longer. I have to leave this place, I've already waited two years.

VOICE OF ZENG HAO *(from outside):* Sufang! Sufang!

SUFANG: Where can you go?

RUIZHEN *(staring into space):* This girlfriend of mine told me that there's a place, where . . .

SUFANG *(sadly and slowly):* But what about your baby? *(Hands Ruizhen the little baby dress.)*

RUIZHEN *(takes the dress and looks at it):* The baby. *(Sighs deeply, and drops the dress on the floor.)*

(Zeng Hao's upper torso can be seen through the study door.)

HAO *(raises the candle):* Sufang, the water bag's leaking. My whole bed is wet.

(Sufang and Zeng Hao exit through the study door. Siyi enters, with an account book, from her bedroom, while Ruizhen quickly picks up and hides the little dress.)

SIYI *(catches a glimpse of Sufang's back):* Su Meimei! Su Meimei! *(to Ruizhen):* Wasn't that your Auntie Su?

RUIZHEN: Uh.

SIYI: Why was she in such a hurry to leave when she saw me come in?

RUIZHEN: Grandfather wants her for something.

SIYI *(harshly):* Go and bring her here, and tell her that your father's looking for her.

(Ruizhen, head lowered, exits through the study door. The night watchman can be heard from a distance. Wenqing enters from the bedroom. Siyi walks up to the table and starts counting money.)

WENQING *(anxiously):* What do you want?

SIYI *(rolls her eyes):* I don't want anything.

WENQING: What are you going to do? Tell me, tell me!

SIYI *(faking obedience and tolerance):* Nothing bothers me anymore. Life is so meaningless. Sooner or late the coffin will be nailed, I'll stretch out my legs, and everything will become unreal. *(Walks toward her bedroom.)*

WENQING: What are you doing?

SIYI *(turns her head):* What am I doing? I'm going to hand this account book over to somebody. *(Walks into the bedroom.)*

WENQING *(facing the bedroom door):* Why do you have to do this? Why do you have to do this? What do you really want? Tell me!

(Siyi reenters from the bedroom, still carrying the account book.)

SIYI *(rolling her eyes):* I don't want anything. All I want is that in the future you just don't forget how well this honest person's treated you. Bright and early tomorrow morning I'm moving into a nunnery. I've already sent word.

WENQING: Oh, heavens. Please be honest with me. What's really on your mind? I'm no stranger to you. We've been together now for twenty years. Why are you doing this?

SIYI *(takes out the letter that Sufang has given Wenqing earlier; sneeringly):* Humph! She must think that I'm some sort of pushover. She even had the nerve to hand poems and letters to you right in front of my eyes. *(Suddenly becomes malicious.)* One more thing, I want you to give this letter back to her right here in front of me.

WENQING *(evasively):* I, I'm going to leave tomorrow.

SIYI *(severely):* Then you give it back to her right now. I've already sent for her.

WENQING *(frightened):* What, what for?

SIYI *(sarcastically):* Oh, to come for the love letters you have for her!

WENQING *(despairingly):* Oh! *(About to turn and run back to their bedroom.)*

SIYI *(harshly):* Where do you think you're going?

(Wenqing stops.)

SIYI *(sneeringly):* A mouse that can't even steal oil shouldn't drool in front of a cat. I'm going to show her . . .

(Suddenly the lights go out in the living room; the huge shadow vanishes. Yuan Yuan has changed into her pajamas when she opens and enters through a section of the folding door. She is cradling Solitude

[the pigeon], holding a candle in one hand and a piece of paper in the other.)

YUAN *(vivaciously):* Hey *(hands the letter to Wenqing),* Uncle Zeng, a letter from my father! *(Turns to face Siyi, pointing):* The two of you are still up; we're going to bed now. *(Turns and exits, skipping into the living room, as the door quickly shuts behind her.)*

WENQING *(lets out a long sigh after reading Mr. Yuan's letter):* Ai.

SIYI: What is it?

WENQING *(hands her the letter):* Mr. Yuan said his fiancée will be here any day now.

SIYI: He has a fiancée?

WENQING: Yes, and he wants you to find them a nice place to live.

SIYI *(finishes reading the letter; sarcastically):* Mm . . . in that case, our good Miss Su is going to . . .

(Sufang enters through the study door, holding a candle.)

SUFANG *(softly):* Did you want to see me, Cousin Wenqing?

WENQING: I . . .

SIYI: Yes, Su Mei. *(Hands the letter to Wenqing.)* Well?

WENQING: Oh! *(Wants to leave.)*

SIYI *(harshly):* Stay right where you are! Do you want me to really lose my temper?

WENQING *(pleading sadly):* Sufang, you'd better leave. Don't listen to her.

(Sufang turns and looks at Siyi, then starts to turn around.)

SIYI *(to Sufang):* Don't move! *(To Wenqing, wickedly):* Take this and give it back to her.

(Wenqing takes the letter from her in defeat. Sufang looks at Wenqing uncomfortably and stands stiffly.)

SIYI *(grins malignantly):* I suppose this is the letter you wrote Wenqing? Wenqing says he cannot accept the honor, so would you please take it back.

(Sufang takes the letter from Wenqing in her shaking hands. Wenqing lowers his head. Silence. Sufang exits quietly through the study door.

Wenqing turns and follows Sufang's exit with his eyes, then collapses on the sofa and starts weeping.)

SIYI *(cruelly, softly):* What are you crying about, did your father just die or something?

WENQING *(shakes his head):* Don't torture me like this, I can't take it much longer.

SIYI *(sighs deeply):* The Du family's bookkeeper came over to ask for their money again tonight. The old man's still holding on to that bankbook of his. He's not parting with a cent! Wenqing, let's see which one of us is going to die first; these people are driving me mad. *(Exits hurriedly through the study door.)*

(Wenqing, still beside himself, stands up and walks slowly toward his bedroom. A sudden loud noise can be heard behind the door of the bedroom on the other side of the parlor, as if a stick has been thrown against the door. Wencai rushes in from her bedroom, crying as she runs.)

WENCAI *(fearfully in a low voice):* Brother!

WENQING: What happened?

WENCAI: He's on a rampage again!

WENQING *(feebly):* Then, I, what can I do?

WENCAI *(anxiously):* Brother, what should we do now? What should we do?

(Suddenly a sound of things being smashed is heard from the same bedroom, followed by the snarling voice of a person cursing.)

WENCAI *(holds onto Wenqing's arm):* Did you hear that? He's breaking things again.

WENQING *(holds his head in both hands):* Ai, let him do it!

WENCAI *(painfully):* He, he's gone mad. He was going to hit me, he wanted to divorce me . . .

WENQING *(smiles tragically):* Divorce you?

VOICE OF JIANG TAI *(from the bedroom, pounding the table):* Wencai! Wencai!

WENCAI: Brother.

VOICE OF JIANG TAI *(from the bedroom, still pounding on the table and yelling):* Wencai! Wencai! Wencai!

WENCAI *(holds onto Wenqing):* Brother, listen!

WENQING: Let go of me!

WENCAI *(worriedly):* He's dangerous! Brother, he's going to do something crazy!

WENQING: Leave me alone. I've got my own problems. *(Shakes off Wencai's hands, and staggers into his own bedroom.)*

(Wencai takes a couple of steps toward her own bedroom when the door is suddenly thrown open. A drunken Jiang Tai stumbles in, with a slipper on one foot and the other bare.)

JIANG *(the pitiful expression that he wore on his face earlier has all but vanished; he leans against the door frame with his bloodshot eyes wide open):* Where the hell have you been? Do you know who I am? My name is Jiang Tai. I called you, I called you, why didn't you come?

WENCAI *(painfully):* I, I, you . . .

JIANG: I don't live here in your house without paying my dues! I've been pushed around by other people my whole life. When I'm home, do I have to take this nonsense from all of you? I get whatever I want around here. If I want to drink, somebody should get it for me. If I want something to eat, somebody should make it for me. If anyone tries to pull one over on me, I'll take care of them— Let's go— *(grasps Wencai's hand)* get him!

WENCAI *(blocks his way):* Who are you looking for?

JIANG: Zeng Hao, your father, he owes me an apology. I'm going to set things straight with him!

WENCAI: Tomorrow, we'll do that tomorrow. Father's sleeping now.

JIANG: Then tell him to get the hell up right now. *(Starts walking.)*

WENCAI *(tries to restrain him):* No, don't go!

JIANG: You keep out of this!

WENCAI *(an idea dawns on her suddenly; turns her head):* Oh, look, Father's here now!

JIANG: Where?

WENCAI: Here! (*She eases Jiang Tai toward their bedroom door and suddenly pushes him inside, immediately locking the door.*)

VOICE OF JIANG TAI (*from the bedroom, pounding on the door*): Open the door! Open the door!

WENCAI: Brother! (*Quickly runs over to Wenqing's bedroom.*) Brother!

VOICE OF JIANG TAI (*from the bedroom, pounding on the door*): Open the door! Open the door!

(*Wencai goes to Wenqing's door and lifts the door curtain.*)

WENCAI (*as if seeing something frightful*): Oh, God! You're still smoking that!

VOICE OF WENQING (*in his bedroom*): Don't bother me. You suffer; I suffer too.

VOICE OF JIANG TAI (*in his bedroom, screaming and yelling*): Wencai! (*Pounds on the door furiously.*) If you don't open the door, I'll burn the house down! I'll burn the house down, I'm starting the fire, I . . .

(*A thump, as if Jiang Tai has fallen flat on the floor.*)

WENCAI (*simultaneously runs toward her own bedroom, screaming*): Oh my God, Jiang Tai, wake up! Haven't you started enough trouble?! And now you want to frighten me to death! (*Opens the door.*)

(*Wencai instantly rushes into her bedroom and slams the door behind her. The sound of Jiang Tai moaning and groaning can be heard from inside. Zeng Hao enters through the study door, helped by Sufang. With a thin robe over his shoulders, he is shivering. He carries a lantern.*)

HAO (*nervously*): What happened? What happened? (*To Sufang in a low voice*): Let, let me go and see who, who's making all this noise! Hurry now and bring me my quilted robe.

(*Sufang exits through the study door. Jiang Tai is still moaning in his bedroom. Zeng Hao, catching a glimpse of the light in Wenqing's bedroom, walks quietly toward the door, lifts the curtain and looks inside.*)

VOICE OF WENQING (*from the bedroom, hoarsely*): Who's there?

HAO: Who's there? *(As if struck by some unimaginable force):* What? You, you haven't left yet?

(Wenqing is petrified, but somehow manages to enter slumberously with his opium pipe.)

HAO: Why, why you're smoking again! . . .

WENQING *(head lowered):* Father, I . . .

(Zeng Hao is so shocked that he cannot speak. When he staggers toward Wenqing, Wenqing timidly retreats to the dining table. Suddenly Zeng Hao falls on his knees before Wenqing.)

HAO *(heartbroken):* I'm kneeling before you. I beg of you as if you were my father and I were your son! I beg of you to stop smoking. I will kowtow to you if you would only . . . *(Starts to kowtow).*

WENQING *(suddenly realizes the intense and deepening effect of his sin, throws down the opium-pipe):* Oh, my God! *(Throws open the living room folding door and runs out.)*

(Simultaneously, Zeng Hao suffers a stroke and falls near the sofa. At the same time, Sufang enters through the study door with the quilted robe. Seeing what has happened to Zeng Hao, she rushes to his side.)

SUFANG *(frightened):* Uncle! Uncle! *(Helps him to the sofa.)* Uncle, are you all right? Uncle, wake up! Uncle!

HAO *(weakly with half-open eyes):* Is, is he gone?

SUFANG *(trembling):* He's gone.

HAO *(gnashing his teeth):* A son like that ought *(stamps his foot)* to be shot! *(Stamps his foot again.)* Dead! *(Trying to get up, feeling that his tongue is not responding to his command.)* My tongue . . . is all . . . numb . . . you . . .

SUFANG *(her voice trembling):* Uncle, sit down. I'll bring your ginseng soup, Uncle!

(Zeng Hao, with his mouth and eyes wide open, is unable to respond. Sufang rushes out through the study door.)

VOICE OF WENCAI *(from the bedroom, crying):* Jiang Tai! Jiang Tai!

VOICE OF JIANG TAI *(from the same bedroom, roaring):* Get away from me!

VOICE OF WENCAI: Jiang Tai!

(Jiang Tai quickly opens the door and immediately locks it behind him.)

VOICE OF WENCAI *(from the bedroom):* Open the door! Open the door!

JIANG *(in the flickering light of the candle, sees Zeng Hao sitting there as if in meditation and says angrily):* Oh, so you're meditating here!

(Zeng Hao still has his mouth and eyes wide open.)

JIANG: You don't have to stare at me like that, I'm definitely leaving tomorrow! I'm definitely leaving! Even if I don't get rich I can still feed my own wife. *(Angrily and bitterly.)* But before I go, you and I have got to set things straight.

VOICE OF WENCAI *(from the bedroom, yelling anxiously):* Open the door! Open the door! Jiang Tai, who're you talking to?! *(Pounds on the door.)* Open up, Jiang Tai! Open the door! *(Continues to yell whenever Jiang Tai pauses.)*

JIANG: You have to pay back what you owe me. I've never brought this up before, but you can't play dumb with me anymore. Because of you I lost my job with the government; because of you, I got involved in an embezzlement. Now the law's out to get me. My reputation's ruined. I'll never be anybody for the rest of my life. That's what you owe me, and that's what you're going to pay me back for. You can't just brush me aside as easily as that! You're going to give me one more chance! Don't just sit there and say nothing. Do you know who I am? I'm your son-in-law, Jiang Tai. I'm Jiang Tai! You owe me money. Zeng Hao, Zeng Hao, do you hear me?

VOICE OF WENCAI *(from the bedroom, frightened):* Open the door! Open the door! *(Yells continuously.)* Father! Father! Don't pay any attention to him! He's just talking nonsense, he's insane! Father, Father, oh Father! Open the door, Jiang Tai! *(Inserted between Jiang Tai's speeches.)* Open the door! Father! Father!

JIANG: Zeng Hao, are you going to pay up or not? Are you going to pay me back? I know all about your savings, all that gold, silver, all your stocks and real estate. *(Suddenly begs.)* Oh, just loan me three thousand dollars, only three thousand, I could go into business, and after I make a little profit, I'll pay you back, with interest too. Did you hear me? I'll pay you double! Old Master Zeng, it's Jiang Tai talking to you. What are you sitting on that money for? You're an old man and you're not getting any younger. Your coffin's all ready for you. It's been lacquered several hundred times, you . . .

VOICE OF WENCAI *(pounding on the door as Jiang Tai speaks):* Open the door! Open the door!

(Siyi enters angrily through the study door, holding Zeng Hao's red bankbook. She glances at Zeng Hao momentarily, walks over to Wencai's bedroom, and opens the door.)

JIANG *(unaware that someone has walked in, still looks at Zeng Hao and says loathingly):* What are you laughing at? What are you laughing at me for? *(Suddenly very fiercely):* Why haven't you died yet? Oh, why don't you die? *(Madly rushes up to Zeng Hao, and shakes the shoulders of the unconscious old man.)*

(Wencai rushes in from her bedroom, with tears running down her face.)

WENCAI *(tries to pull Jiang Tai away; screams in an exhausted and hoarse voice):* You monster! You devil!

JIANG *(being pulled by Wencai toward his own bedroom, but still shouting in great agitation):* Let me go, let me go! I'm going to kill someone, I'm going to kill him, and then I'm going to kill myself.

(Wencai finally succeeds in dragging Jiang Tai back into the bedroom, and slams the door shut. Sufang hurries in through the study door with the ginseng soup. Siyi still stands by with disgust on her face.)

SUFANG *(feeding the ginseng soup to Zeng Hao):* Uncle! Uncle! Drink a little of this, Uncle!

(Zeng Ting runs in through the study door.)

TING: What happened?

SUFANG *(unable to feed Zeng Hao the soup):* Grandfather's in bad shape. Hurry up and phone Dr. Luo.

TING: What's wrong?

SUFANG: He's had a stroke! Uncle! Uncle!

(Zeng Ting runs out through the living room door as Chen Naima hurries in through the study door, still putting her clothes on.)

CHEN *(trembling):* What happened to the Old Master? Is the Old Master all right?

SUFANG *(urgently):* Come and hold his head up. I'm going to force it down.

(The phlegm begins welling up in the old man's throat.)

CHEN *(holding his head):* No, no, oh my God! There's too much phlegm in his throat . . . his jaw is locked tight. We'll never get it down.

SUFANG: Uncle! Uncle!

(Wenqing enters through the living room door.)

WENQING *(walks up to the old man and cries aloud in shame):* Oh Father! Oh Father! It's all my fault! It's all my fault!

(Wencai runs in from her own bedroom.)

WENCAI *(clutching his knee):* Father, Father, oh my Father!

SUFANG: Uncle! Uncle!

CHEN: Old Master! Old Master!

SIYI *(suddenly):* Stop this screaming and yelling! Send him to the hospital now, we can't wait for the doctor.

SUFANG *(protesting):* But Uncle doesn't want to go to the hospital.

SIYI *(to Chen Naima):* Get someone over here!

(Chen Naima exits through the living room door.)

WENCAI *(hurriedly):* I'll go next door and borrow the Dus' car.
    (Runs out through the living room door.)

SUFANG: Uncle, Uncle!

WENQING *(sobbing):* What are we going to do? What are we going to do?

SIYI: Humph, what are we going to do? *(Throws Zeng Hao's red bankbook in front of Wenqing, angrily.)* See for yourself!

(Chen Naima leads Zhang Shun through the living room door. Zeng Ting enters behind them.)

SIYI: Where's Zhang Shun?

CHEN: He's right here.

SIYI *(to Zhang Shun):* Carry him to the car.

(Zhang Shun is about to lift the Old Master.)

SUFANG *(suddenly clutching at Zeng Hao):* We'll never get him to the hospital in time. I don't think Uncle's going to make it.

(The old man cannot speak but looks on in pain. Zhang Shun looks at Sufang and stops.)

SIYI *(pulls Sufang away; to Zhang Shun):* Go on.

(Zhang Shun lifts Zeng Hao and carries him toward the living room.)

TING *(starts crying):* Grandfather! Grandfather!

SIYI: Stop crying!

WENQING *(follows Zeng Hao):* Father, it's all my fault.

(As soon as Zhang Shun reaches the threshold, the pale hand of the old man suddenly grasps the folding doors, unwilling to let go.)

TING *(turns):* Grandfather won't let go of the door.

SIYI: Use your strength!

SUFANG *(grievously):* Oh, he doesn't want to leave home. *(Everyone hesitates momentarily.)*

SIYI: Hurry up, hurry! His life is in danger. Who's giving the orders around here, me or her? Carry him out!

(Zhang Shun forces his way forward.)

SUFANG: His hand, his hand!

SIYI *(to Ting):* Pry his hand away.

TING: I'm scared.

SIYI: Let me do it, stupid.

WENQING: Father! Father!

TING *(points, horrified):* Look at Grandfather's hand! Look at Grandfather's hand!

(Siyi forcibly pries Zeng Hao's hand loose.)

WENQING *(furious):* You witch! You've cut his hand!

SIYI: Move him! *(Maliciously, in a low voice):* We're going to sell this house. Do you want someone to die here?

(All of them, except Wenqing, follow Zhang Shun and exit through the living room door. The night-watchman's clap. Sound of the hoarse voice of the "noodle cake" peddler. A painful, drunken moan can be heard coming from the bedroom. Wenqing enters his bedroom and immediately

walks out again, carrying an old jacket and a battered hat, with a scroll under his arm. He lets out a long sigh and exits slowly through the living room door, closing it behind him. The autumn rain is swept into the parlor by a draft. The living room door quietly opens by itself as the glow of candlelight casts flickering shadows on the walls. Stirred by the draft, the hanging scroll bangs against the wall. Outside the lonely gong of the night watchman can be heard in the distance.)

Slow curtain

Act 3

Scene 1

Toward the end of the ninth lunar month, people in Peking are already wearing winter clothes during the cooler hours. The late autumn sky is exceptionally peaceful and clear. In the older gardens, as dusk approaches one can see flocks of crows circling over the old elm trees like dots of ink, cawing endlessly at each other. Later, when darkness begins to fall, the crows return to their nests. In the sea of evening mist, one hears the bugle of a diligent soldier high up on the city wall. Distant and solitary, it touches the deepest recesses of men's hearts with its mixture of warmth and loneliness, like a sentimental spirit in lonely pursuit of memories of a past forever vanished. Remorseful, mournful, filled with bitter but tender yearnings, it trembles as it passes through the chilly dusk air.

The days are getting shorter. It is barely six o'clock, and yet the sun behind the stone arch is already sinking into the haze of lavender mist. Late at night, the strong west wind sweeps through, stirring half-withered trees in the gardens. Yet early the next morning, the sun once again graces the glimmering tiles on the rooftops. The sky is clear, the air is clean, and the ground is covered with white frost. The fallen leaves, ravaged by the wind the previous night, carpet the courtyards and the sidewalks. The weather is growing much colder these days, especially in the early morning hours. The breath of early risers turns to milk-white clouds in the cold air; and vegetables bought from the market are occasionally coated in a thin layer of frost. Those who sit in a room for long find their feet getting numb. Flies struggle as they knock against the paper windows and finally fall weakly on the ledges.

In the past, wealthy families—the Zeng family among them— would by now have fires built. The room would be warm and cozy. Before the partitions that surround the living room and before the huge windows, there would be potted chrysanthemums in every conceivable color: green, white, yellow, both large- and small-petalled, all of them famous varieties. Some pots would be on stands, others on the floor. These would also be the purple thousand-headed chrysanthemum hanging upside down, as if from a steep cliff, from a red sandalwood stand in front of the blue gauze partition. Dazzling, they seemed to compete for one's attention. Occasionally, when the Zengs were in a gay mood, they would sit admiringly before the chrysanthemums and sip wine. They would invite a few close friends to enjoy a hot chafing dish of mutton and would indulge in drinking games and poetry composition. Their ears reddened by the wine, they reveled without a care in the world. It was truly the height of enjoyment.

But now, all traces of the joy of those days are gone from the Zeng house. Gloom has replaced the grandiosity of yesteryear. At dusk of a late autumn day—a little more than a month from the close of act 2— the house is scarred with signs of desolation and neglect. The color of the blue gauze curtains on the partition has faded, and a couple of them have been torn from the panels. They have been replaced by white paper, but that too is already yellowed with age. A pot of white chrysanthemums stands in front of the partition, but the leaves are dry and the flowers have withered. On the half-moon shaped redwood table which stands by the wall, a few lifeless chrysanthemums rest in a big dark-blue vase. Their petals have fallen all over the table. In this rapidly declining family, those drooping flowers somehow symbolize the occasion. Most of the ornaments have been stored. There is a landscape painting on the wall, apparently by an unknown artist. Its mounting has turned a dull gray, and there is only axle left on the roller at the bottom. The wallpaper is beginning to peel. The seven-stringed lute hanging in one corner of the room has lost its case. Its orange silk tassel still hangs from it dumbly, but the color no longer retains its former brilliance. Spiders have woven webs from the lute diagonally up to the ceiling. Some of the torn window papers in the study have been patched over and torn again. Two square stools stand casually along the wall, one empty, the other holding a sewing basket. It seems no one has bothered to clean the octagonal window for some time, as it is covered with dust. A teapot and two teacups rest on the square table, a high-backed chair placed next to it.

The weak glow of the setting sun filters in through the windows, caressing the fallen chrysanthemum petals and the tassel of the web-shrouded lute. The light brightens momentarily, as if announcing its presence to the room, and then quickly dims again. Outside, as the crows caw, the single-wheel water cart passes sounding its same mo-notonous tune: "zhu-niu-niu, zhu-niu-niu." The room darkens as the sun sinks behind the mountains.

As the curtain rises, Wencai is sitting in the high-backed chair knitting a shawl. She is wearing a black flannel gown and a pair of felt shoes. She appears anxious. Every so often she stops knitting as if waiting for something. Far away from her, Jiang Tai is leaning on the sofa totally absorbed in reading The Taoist Physiognomy. *He is hold-ing in his left hand a broken mirror tied together with red wool yarn. While examining himself repeatedly in the mirror, he refers carefully back to the text.*

Time passes.

Chen Naima enters through the study with a shoe sole that she has been stitching. Her hair is whiter, and her face appears more wrinkled. At her age, she is sensitive to the cold. Thus she is already wearing a gray quilted jacket, and a pair of blue satin trousers with the ends tied to her ankles. Wencai sees her, immediately puts down the knitting, and stands up.

WENCAI *(very concerned, in a low voice):* What's happening now? *(Chen Naima stops, turns her head toward the window and listens attentively. Wencai looks at her sadly, awaiting a reply.)*
CHEN *(shakes her head helplessly):* They're still here. They refuse to
    leave.
(Wencai sighs with disappointment, sits down and picks up the shawl, lowers her head, and starts knitting slowly. Jiang Tai turns his head

slightly and glances at the two women. His expression is one of disdain. He goes back to reading his physiognomy text. Chan Naima lets out a long sigh, looks all around her, and dries the corners of her eyes with her sleeve. She walks to the stool and sits down, and in the fading light of the sunset begins silently stitching the shoe sole. Jiang Tai suddenly rubs his uncomfortably cold feet.)

WENCAI *(raises her head and looks at Jiang Tai)*: Are your feet cold?

JIANG *(impatiently)*: Hmm. *(Continues reading his book.)*

(Wencai lowers her head and goes back to her knitting. Momentary silence.)

WENCAI *(glances at Jiang Tai from out of the corner of her eye, lowers her head, and knits two stitches; she is unable to bear it any longer)*: Tai!

(Jiang Tai seems to hear but pays no attention. He continues his reading.)

WENCAI *(kindly)*: What are you doing?

(Jiang Tai ignores her. Chen Naima looks at Jiang Tai briefly and turns her head away in disapproval.)

WENCAI *(puts down her knitting)*: Tai, what time is it now?

JIANG *(picks up the mirror and looks into it without turning his head)*: I don't know.

WENCAI *(looking outside)*: It's probably about six.

JIANG *(puts down the mirror, turns his head, points with his finger, and says coldly)*: There's a clock right here!

WENCAI: That clock is broken.

JIANG *(rolls his eyes)*: If it's broken, then send it out to be repaired. *(Picks up the mirror again.)*

WENCAI *(timidly)*: Tai, please go into the living room and see what they're doing, would you?

JIANG *(Impatiently)*: I don't care, I don't want to be bothered, I can't do anything about it anyway. Your family affairs are too complicated, there's nothing I can do.

WENCAI *(imploring)*: Please go take another look, all right? Find out what the Dus are really up to.

JIANG: What they are up to? They're here to collect money from your family. If you don't have the money, they'll take your house. If you don't give them your house, they'll take Old Master Zeng's coffin, that old cedar box they've been varnishing all these years.

WENCAI *(weakly):* But that coffin is Father's life! His whole life!

JIANG: Since you know how difficult the situation is, why are you asking me to go?

CHEN *(long ago having stopped her sewing to listen, interrupts):* Never mind! Let Da Nainai handle them. Anyway, we have no money and we need the house to live in . . .

JIANG: Then the coffin . . .

WENCAI: Father would never part with it.

JIANG *(glares at Wencai):* Now do you understand? *(Picks up the mirror again.)*

(Wencai lowers her head with a sigh, takes out her handkerchief and dries her tears. Momentary silence. Crows cawing outside. Murmuring sound of the passing water cart—"zhu-niu-niu, zhu-niu-niu.")

CHEN *(stitching the shoe sole, occasionally running the needle through her gray streaked hair, then forcing the needle back into the sole; here she stops, raises her head, and sighs):* I'm leaving, I'm leaving. I'm going to leave tomorrow. What a pity the Old Master has to be so miserable on his birthday. Ai! If he has to go on living like this, wouldn't it have been better if the other night he just . . . *(Suddenly):* In the past when the father of the Old Master celebrated his birthday, the house was full of guests. There was even an opera performance. The garden and the living room were filled with chrysanthemums. There were banquet tables everywhere, and crowds of people came to pay their respects. It seemed as if the whole world were filled with birthday peaches, birthday noodles, bright red wall hangings, nothing like the way it looks now . . .

WENCAI *(contemplating the present difficulties, dumbly staring at Jiang Tai, as if she had heard nothing Chen Naima said; she attempts to compose herself and makes a sincere attempt to talk to Jiang Tai):* Tai, what are you doing?

JIANG *(rolls his eyes):* What do you think I'm doing?

WENCAI *(forces a smile):* What are you looking at in that mirror?

JIANG *(already annoyed, stands up):* I'm looking at my nose! Do you get that? I'm looking at my nose. My nose! My nose! *(Picks up the mirror and the book, walks to another chair and sits down.)*

WENCAI: Don't shout anymore, we should be grateful that Father's still with us.

JIANG *(feeling that Wencai is annoying him intentionally, points at her with a frustrated, helpless look):* Look at you! Look at you! Every time you open your mouth, you're insinuating that I'm the one responsible for your father's illness. But go ask anybody and see who doesn't mention that brother and sister-in-law of yours . . .

WENCAI *(trying to explain):* Who would think of such a thing? *(Lowering her voice and swallowing her pride; tenderly):* What I mean is, Father just came back from the hospital today. Why don't you go up and see him in his room, just this once, on his birthday. All right?

JIANG *(still angry):* I don't understand you. If he doesn't want to see me, why are you trying to force me to go and see him? So, I was drunk that night, said a lot of bad things to him, but I went to see him in the hospital last month. He wouldn't even let me in, he wouldn't see me . . .

WENCAI *(explaining):* Ai! The poor old man is in a bad state now.

JIANG: Well how do you think I feel?

WENCAI *(with difficulty):* But Father is home now; do you mean to say you never want to see him again? Just imagine that we're guests here, and the host just came home, shouldn't we go and say hello, and you . . .

JIANG *(feels caught, but walks up to her arrogantly and points in her face):* You, you, where did you ever pick up that sharp tongue of yours? You're so subtle! I'd better stay away from you. Are you satisfied now? *(In a huff he takes the mirror and exits through the study door.)*

WENCAI *(sadly):* Jiang Tai!

CHEN: Ai! Let him go!

(Jiang Tai hurries back in and begins rummaging about where he was sitting before exit.)

JIANG: Where is my book? *(Rummaging.)* Oh, here it is. *(Exits.)*

WENCAI: Jiang Tai!

CHEN *(very sympathetically):* Ai. Let him go. Better if they don't see each other. If he sees Gu Laoye, the Old Master may very well be reminded about Master Wenqing, and that would make him feel even worse.

WENCAI *(sighs hopelessly):* Have you finished mending that sole?

CHEN *(smiles):* I've got a few more stitches to go. *(Puts down the shoe sole, removes her wire-rimmed glasses, and rubs her eyes.)* The shoes are ready now, but he's not here to wear them.

WENCAI *(forcing optimism):* He'll come back sooner or later.

CHEN *(pauses, and picks up the hem of her gown with both hands and wipes her tears; sorrowfully):* Yes, I really hope so.

WENCAI *(bleakly):* Naima, don't leave tomorrow. Brother will be back in just a few more days.

CHEN *(the troubles of the last month have drained the ruddy glow from her face; her head trembles, and her dry toothless mouth jerks in spasms; in her heart she cannot bear to leave, but she says stubbornly):* No, no, I have to go, I have to go. *(She stands up and puts her needle and thread into her sewing basket while rubbing her red nose.)* I waited and waited . . . I've already waited more than a month. I've made my vows, and burned incense, but we haven't heard a word from him. Poor Master Wenqing, when he left, all he had on was a light jacket . . . *(Calls outside):* Xiao Zhuer! Xiao Zhuer!

WENCAI: Maybe Xiao Zhuer is helping Mr. Yuan with his luggage.

CHEN *(taking a small piece of cloth out of her basket and wrapping up the pair of unfinished cloth shoes):* If, if he comes back one day, let me know as soon as you can, and I'll rush right back from the village to see him. *(Tearfully):* When, when you find out where he is, would you please send this pair of

shoes to him? *(Turns her head and calls again):* Xiao Zhuer!
(To Wencai): Tell him that they were made by his old Naima,
and ask him to send me a note. *(Smiles through her tears.)*
Whenever that is, as long as I'm still around, I'll go to him
no matter how far away he is. *(Cannot help sobbing again.)*

WENCAI *(walks over to console Chen Naima):* Don't, don't be so
upset! He'll be all right out there. *(Forces a smile.)* He's almost thirty-six years old, and he's almost a grandfather.
How could . . .

CHEN *(tears glistening in her eyes):* No matter how old he is, he'll
always be a child to me. He never left home before, and he
still can't even take care of his own food and clothing . . .
(Calling as she walks toward the living room door): Xiao Zhuer!
Xiao Zhuer!

VOICE OF ZIAO ZHUER: Yes? Grandmother!

CHEN: What are you doing now? Go get yourself ready for bed.
We have a long trip tomorrow.

VOICE OF XIAO ZHUER: I'm helping Miss Su feed the pigeon.

CHEN *(walks toward the living room, muttering):* Poor Miss Su! She'll
be here all by herself. What a waste of food. At such a time
why is she still feeding the pigeon?

(Exits through living room door.)

WENCAI *(half talking to Chen Naima and half to herself, sighs):* She's
doing that for someone who really loves pigeons.

*(Crows cawing outside. Wencai shivers and goes on with her knitting.
Jiang Tai enters through study door, looking dejected.)*

JIANG *(abandoning his previous arrogance, as if soaked thoroughly by
a rainstorm on a gloomy afternoon, he shakes his head in an inex-
pressable combination of despondence, anger, and sorrow):* I give
up! I give up! I GIVE UP! In a house as big as this, no matter
where you go, you can't find even one warm spot. It's winter already, and they still haven't put on the heat. I'm freez-
ing my feet off. All your sister-in-law knows is how to
squeeze money out of people! All your father cares about is

his coffin. I really can't see what's the use of living here like this. What's the use?

WENCAI: Stop complaining. No matter how difficult things get, we must go on.

JIANG: When I'm totally bored to death, I'll join the revolution too! (*From half joking and letting off steam, he gradually begins shouting in anger.*) I'll join the resistance, I'll revolt, I'll go make friends in the revolutionary party just like little Ruizhen. We'll resist and attack, attack and resist! The hell with it! We'll overthrow the whole bunch of them! We're going to start this revolution right now! But . . . (*Suddenly puts his hand into his pocket, realizing that he is about to make a fool of himself, laughing nervously.*) But I've only got a dollar left to my name (*feeling around in his pocket and blinking his eyes*). No, I even spent my last dollar (*rolls his eyes, thinking, in a low voice*) on a fortune-teller!

WENCAI: Jiang Tai, you . . .

JIANG (*suddenly shaking his head dejectedly, emits a long deep sigh*): Wouldn't it be great if I could only invent something like Tiger Balm Oil? That would be great!

WENCAI (*mournfully*): Tai, stop talking gibberish. If you keep on like that, you'll drive yourself crazy.

JIANG (*as if he hasn't heard her, suddenly pulling himself together*): Wencai, let me tell you. I was walking around in the market this morning, and I went to see a fortune-teller. He told me that my nose, because of its placement and fullness, is perfect for storing up wealth. (*Very seriously*): I was just looking at this nose of mine myself, really it isn't bad at all! (*Fearing Wencai's reprimand.*) There must be some truth in that kind of fortune-telling—otherwise, how could he have known so much about my past?

WENCAI: Then you should go get in touch with some of your friends.

JIANG (*somewhat self-confident*): Yes! I'll do that, I'll look up some of those rich classmates of mine. *(Encourages himself with his own words.)* I'll find them, I'll get in touch with them right away. I think, this time, I'm really going to do it right.

WENCAI *(encouraging him):* Jiang Tai, all you have to do is put in a little effort, and you're bound to succeed.

JIANG *(joyfully):* Really? *(Suddenly):* Wencai, I just went to see your father in his room.

WENCAI *(also happily):* What, what did he say to you?

JIANG *(cleverly):* It isn't my fault if he wasn't there.

WENCAI: He went out again?

JIANG: Yes, I don't know where he . . .

(Chen Naima enters through the study door.)

CHEN *(somewhat anxiously):* Gu Xiaojie,[1] go look at him!

WENCAI: What's the matter?

CHEN: Ai! The Old Master took his cane and went back to the storeroom by himself to look at his coffin.

WENCAI: Oh . . .

CHEN *(painfully):* The Old Master's in there all by himself, standing right in front of the coffin and crying.

JIANG: Where's Miss Su?

CHEN: Maybe she's making soup for Da Nainai in the kitchen . . . Gu Xiaojie, that coffin should never be given to the Du family no matter what. You'd better go and try to talk to the Old Master.

WENCAI *(tearfully):* Poor Father! I'll go . . . *(Walks toward the study.)*

JIANG *(sarcastically):* No, Wencai, why don't you go and try to talk to your dear sister-in-law first?

WENCAI *(seriously):* But, she's right in the middle of getting the Dus to drop the whole matter.

JIANG: Drop the whole matter? No, she's in there trying to appease the Dus by handing the coffin over to them. Why

---

[1]A respectful way of addressing a daughter of the patriarch, usually a younger, unmarried woman. But Chen finds it appropriate to use this address for Wencai because she is the younger sister of Wenqing and still living in her father's household.

don't you tell her to have a little heart. Tell her not to try so hard to hold onto this mortgaged house. If we wait until she finds a bid high enough to satisfy her, it'll be too late to bring up your father's coffin. Don't forget, when your father left the hospital today, Miss Su paid all his medical bills out of her own pocket. Meanwhile, your sister-in-law's locked herself in her own room feasting on chicken, crying poor, and treating us all like suckers. Do your remember the day your father went into the hospital, it was she who cut his hand and made it bleed? Oh, that honorable sister-in-law of yours . . .

(Siyi enters through the study door.)

CHEN *(hears the footsteps, turns and looks, warns in a low voice):* Da Nainai is coming!

(Jiang Tai falls silent and walks to the other side of the room. Siyi has a glum expression on her face, knits her eyebrows, appears totally penitent. She is wearing a coffee-colored long-sleeved "qi pao" dress embroidered with black flowers. The elbow section of the dress is a bit worn, and the collar unbuttoned. She also has a pair of blue felt shoes.)

WENCAI *(timidly):* What happened, Da Sao![2]

(Siyi walks to the sofa without saying a word. Momentary silence.)

CHEN *(concerned and nervous):* Did the Dus agree or not?

(Siyi sits on the sofa in silence.)

WENCAI: Da Sao, the Dus . . .

SIYI *(suddenly throws herself into the armrest of the sofa and cries):* Wenqing, where are you now? Wenqing, when you ran away, you left all the problems of this family in my hands. What do you expect me to do? If you were here, at least we could talk things over. But you're gone. How do you expect a mere housewife like me to deal with all these headaches?

(Jiang Tai stands to the side, staring coolly at her.)

CHEN *(touched by her outburst):* Da Nainai, tell us, are they going to let us pay later?

---

[2]A common way of addressing the wife of one's oldest brother.

SIYI *(drying her tears and her nose, but still sniffling):* Just think, the Du family has their own textile factory. They are shrewd businessmen. Now that they've backed us into a corner, why should they give up? They know as well as we do that there isn't a man in the house. *(Jiang Tai grunts contemptuously.)* We're all either too old or too young, no wonder they've taken advantage of us and forced us into going along with them. They won't give up!

WENCAI *(hopelessly):* In that case, do they insist on taking father's coffin?

SIYI *(still wiping her swollen eyes with her handkerchief, shoulders quivering as she cries):* What can I do? We don't have any money to give them, we have to live in this house, and there're all these mouths to feed. Old Master Du has had his eyes on that coffin for years, and now, he's insisting that . . .

JIANG *(leaning against the door of his own bedroom, cynically):* Well then, why don't we send it over there . . .

CHEN *(surprised):* What? Send it over there?

SIYI *(ignoring Jiang Tai):* Not only that, they want it today!

WENCAI *(shocked):* Today?

SIYI: Yes. They say Old Master Du is going to die anytime now and in his will, it's stated that . . .

JIANG *(speaking for her):* He must have Old Master Zeng's coffin!

WENCAI *(instantly):* Father would never allow this.

CHEN *(interrupting):* Even if he were willing, who would mention it to him?

WENCAI *(immediately follows):* But Father just came back from the hospital.

CHEN *(interrupts):* And today is also Old Master's birthday . . .

SIYI *(suddenly starts crying again):* Oh, Wenqing, where are you? What can I do? I have to take care of my father-in-law. I have to feed all the members of this family. I can't possibly fulfill all my obligations to them now. Wenqing, what do you want me to do?

(*While Siyi cries, the door of the study opens, Zeng Hao enters shakily, supporting himself with his cane. He is wearing an indigo blue padded gown, a black wool jacket, and black felt shoes. His worried face is yellow and emaciated, but from the way he walks he seems to have recovered. He is trying to maintain his dwindling dignity. From his eyes one can tell that he is mounting a final struggle amid all the hopelessness surrounding him, and that he despises all the people there. They all turn their heads in his direction and stand up. As soon as Jiang Tai notices Hao, he creeps along the wall and slips into his own bedroom.*)

WENCAI: Father! (*Runs over to help him.*)

HAO (*waves her away, trying to raise his weakened voice*): I don't need any help, I can walk by myself. (*Walks toward the sofa.*)

SIYI (*most considerate*): Let me help you back to your room, Father. You should be resting now.

HAO (*sits on the sofa and addresses all present*): Sit down everyone, no need for all this formality . . .

HAO (*looks around*): Where's Jiang Tai?

WENCAI: He . . . (*suddenly recalls*) He's in his bedroom. (*Ashamed*): He's waiting for you Father. He wants to apologize to you.

HAO: Is there any word from Wenqing?

SIYI (*sadly*): Someone said they ran into him on the street in Jinan, then someone else said they saw him in a small inn in Tianjin . . .

WENCAI: We've tried to find him everywhere, but he seems to have vanished without a trace.

HAO: Then don't bother looking anymore.

WENCAI (*makes a special effort to comfort the old man*): I'm sure Brother was so ashamed of himself that this time he'll go out there and make a career for himself before he . . .

HAO (*shaking his head*): "Nobody knows a son better than his father." He doesn't have enough will power. Sooner or later he'll . . . (*Dismissing the subject, suddenly addressing Wencai*): Why don't you go ask Jiang Tai to come in.

WENCAI (*takes a step; turns to her father suddenly*): Father, we, we're all terribly ashamed of ourselves, Father, really . . .

HAO: Ai! Go and get him. You don't have to say all that. *(To Siyi):* Go and bring Ting and Ruizhen here too.

(Wencai goes up to the bedroom door and calls; Siyi exits through the study door.)

WENCAI: Jiang Tai! Jiang . . .

(Jiang Tai immediately enters quietly.)

JIANG *(notices that Zeng Hao has been looking at him from the moment he reappears, ashamed in spite of himself):* Father, you . . .

HAO *(motioning to him):* Sit down, sit down.

(Jiang Tai sits.)

HAO *(to Chen Naima with concern):* Go tell Miss Su to rest a little. She just came back from the hospital. Tell her not to do hard work in the kitchen.

(Chen Naima exits through the living room door.)

WENCAI *(all along gesturing to Jiang Tai, and as Chen Naima turns her back, begins in a low voice):* Get up and apologize to Father!

JIANG *(hesitantly, half standing):* I, I . . .

HAO *(waves his hand):* Never mind. Things pass. Let's not talk about it.

(Jiang Tai sits down again. During the ensuing silence, Siyi enters, leading Ting and Ruizhen, through the study door. Ruizhen is wearing a gray cotton gown decorated with small red flowers. Ting is wearing a long gown with a blue cotton jacket. Zeng Hao points at the chairs. They all sit down in their appropriate places [according to family rank], except for Ruizhen, who is standing behind Wencai.)

HAO *(looks around sorrowfully):* The whole Zeng family is here now, except for Wenqing. *(Looks around the room and coughs lightly.)* This house was passed down to us by your great grandfather Jingde. For generations, ours has been a family of scholars—the fathers kind and the sons filial. All the sons of the Zeng family have been held in the highest esteem by the community until now, when one worthless, unfilial offspring like myself came along.

SIYI *(pained and sorry for him):* Father! . . .

(All stare at each other solemnly, then lower their heads.)

HAO: The reputation of the Zeng family—ruined! I have brought up a bunch of stupid, lazy, unfilial children who can't even hold on to the little we have . . .

(Jiang Tai begins to get impatient.)

WENCAI *(looks up, ashamed):* Father, father, you . . .

HAO: I have been a great disappointment to my ancestors, and I can only tremble at the thought of seeing my father Jingde Gong again *(coughs).*

(Ruizhen walks over and starts massaging his back.)

JIANG *(impatient, turns away shaking his head, sighs, and mutters):* At a time like this, what's the use of putting on such a big show? What's the use?

WENCAI *(in a low voice):* Are you at it again?

HAO *(gently pushes Ruizhen's hands away):* Don't bother now. *(Turns toward the rest):* I'm not blaming you. That wouldn't do any good. *(With a hopeless expression on his face, and in a hostile tone of voice):* What a bunch of stupid idiots, what a bunch of useless, big-mouthed fools! *(Suddenly gathering courage)* Jiang Tai you too . . .

(Jiang Tai is about to reply.)

WENCAI *(on the alert):* Tai!

(Jiang Tai falls silent.)

HAO *(half scolding, half complaining):* You sit around all day thinking you're going to strike it rich. Day-dreaming. You don't know a thing about the outside world. You're just like Wenqing. All that studying for nothing, I don't know what's gotten into you two, you're just a pair of . . . *(Starts to cough and rubs his chest.)*

WENCAI: Ai! Ai!

JIANG *(forcing himself to respond):* What's the use? What's the use?

WENCAI: Father, Father!

HAO: Siyi, you are a mother and your son's been married for two years. In fact, you'll soon become a grandmother yourself. *(Tries to suppress his own anger.)* I can't blame you because these problems began with me, and they didn't begin today.

(Increasingly more self-pitying.) After you sell the house, you can start pretending that I'm dead, that I don't exist that I, I . . . *(on the verge of tears.)*

WENCAI *(bursts into tears):* Father! Father!

SIYI *(expression already changed):* Father, I don't understand what you are talking about.

HAO *(surprised):* You, you . . .

WENCAI *(furious):* Da Sao, how dare you insult Father like that!

SIYI *(returning the question):* Like what?

WENCAI *(forced to respond):* How can anyone be so heartless?

SIYI: Who's heartless? Tell me who? May Heaven strike me dead, and right here before our father's face, tell me, who, who?

TING *(painfully):* Mother!

WENCAI *(belittled by Siyi's presumptuousness, she trembles in anger):* You're forcing Father right to the edge of a cliff.

JIANG *(powerlessly):* Stop arguing, both of you!

WENCAI: You've even forced your father to sell his own coffin! You've made him . . .

HAO *(stops her):* Wencai!

SIYI *(sarcastically):* You're right. It was I who pushed Father over the edge. I'm the one who's been living off him *(gets up)* like a parasite for the last four years, and I've even brought my husband along for the ride! . . .

TING *(has been trying to stop her, extremely agitated):* Mother! Please don't! Mother, you . . .

JIANG *(upset):* You liar! I've paid my share!

HAO *(wheezing, tries to stop them):* Stop this screaming!

SIYI *(simultaneously):* You paid your share? Humph, you're . . .

HAO *(stamps his foot angrily during the argument):* Siyi, stop it! *(In a wail):* I, I'm dying!

(Everyone stops suddenly; only Siyi's sobbing can be heard. It begins to darken outside. In this solemn atmosphere, Sufang enters through the living room door. She is wearing a beige serge gown, and her face appears somewhat more drawn than a month ago. Her eyes are bigger and brighter, but she is more calm, settled, and relaxed. She holds a

kerosene lamp in her right hand and carries two scrolls under her left arm. As she enters, Ruizhen hurries up to her and takes the lamp from her. She whispers something hurriedly in Sufang's ear. Sufang nods in silence, and looks tragically at the solemn faces in front of her. She places the two scrolls in an urn and then exits quickly through the study door. Ruizhen has followed her every movement with her eyes.)

HAO *(sighs)*: You're all a bunch of idiots! What's the use of arguing at a time like this?

RUIZHEN: Grandfather, you should go to your room and rest!

HAO *(touched)*: Aren't you people ashamed of yourselves, arguing like this in front of Ruizhen and Ting? *(Emotionally)*: Let's forget about it all now. Our days together are numbered. Siyi, go, you go tell the Dus' housekeeper, tell him . . . *(with difficulty)* tell him to take my coffin away! But, but *(bleakly)* leave, leave us the house!

WENCAI: Father!

HAO: Sufang told me what they wanted.

WENCAI: Who asked her to tell you that?

SIYI *(about to start a quarrel)*: Me!

HAO: Let's not think about petty things like this.

JIANG *(hesitantly)*: Then you're really going to give it to them? *(Zeng Hao nods.)*

SIYI *(unwilling to break the news, but finally revealing)*: But they said that they want it today.

HAO: All right, all right. Whatever! Let those blessed sleep in it. *(Siyi is about to exit, when suddenly Zeng Hao turns to Jiang Tai)*: Jiang Tai, go tell them to take it away now, right now! *(In agony)*: I, I never want to see that godforsaken thing again! *(Lowers his head in silence. Siyi stands in place.)*

JIANG *(suddenly sympathetic)*: Father! *(Takes a couple of steps and stops.)*

HAO: Go ahead, go tell them!

JIANG *(suddenly turns around and walks up to Zeng Hao, speaking with kindness)*: Father, there's really no need to get all upset about this! When a person dies, he just dies. What's the difference if the coffin they put you in has been lacquered hundreds of times? *(Gets carried away as he talks; his sympathetic consolation immediately reverts to his old form, as he continues his endless chatter.)* You don't seem to understand. Let's say they put you in a coffin with only one coat of lacquer on it; what does it matter?

WENCAI *(realizes that he is going to make a speech again)*: Jiang Tai!

JIANG *(turns to Wencai loathingly)*: Be quiet! *(Turns back to Zeng Hao and tries seriously to persuade him, in a pleasant manner.)* Now what's the difference if you don't have a coffin at all when you die? *(Gesturing and pointing)*: This is only a kind of custom, a point of view! *(Inspired by his own words, he gradually forgets his original benevolent intention, now gesturing dramatically.)* For example *(sits on the sofa)*, I look good sitting like this, *(gets a clever idea)* but if I *(suddenly rests his leg on the back off the sofa)* sit like this, don't I look good too? *(To Siyi)*: Da Sao. *(Totally absorbed in his own words, speaks to Siyi as if he were slightly intoxicated. By now seems to have forgotten about their recent argument.)* This is only an example! *(Points at her.)* You look good with clothes on; but don't you look good without them as well?

SIYI: Gu Laoye!

JIANG *(talks incessantly)*: I don't think there's any difference, none at all! It's only a matter of opinion, a matter of habit!

HAO *(tries to interrupt)*: Jiang Tai!

JIANG *(not allowing interruption, chatters on)*: Now take me for instance *(sits down again)*. When I die *(turns to Wencai seriously, but nobody knows whether he is joking)* I want to be cremated! Then you can throw my ashes into the sea and have a seaburial. It's the finest cemetery in the world, and best of all, it's free! *(As if he is lecturing a class.)* Now this is only a matter of opinion. This can also become a custom! Then, Father, if you . . .

HAO *(cannot stand it any longer; raises his voice in order to stop him)*: Jiang Tai! The way you want to die and the way you want

to be buried is your own business. *(Bitterly):* I just got over
a serious illness, and no matter what, today is still my birthday. You can save your opinion for . . .

JIANG *(unaffected by the rebuff; still peacefully):* All right. All right.
You don't agree! That doesn't matter! We all have our own
preference . . . Actually from the very beginning I knew I
was wasting my time trying to persuade you. As I was talking to you a while ago, I kept on saying to myself, "Don't
say it! Don't say it!" *(Apologetically),* but I couldn't help myself . . .

SIYI *(has appeared rueful all along):* In that case, Gu Laoye, let's
stop here. *(Stands up.)* Then, Father, I'll, I'll *(seems unwilling
to continue, wipes the corners of her eyes)* follow your instructions and talk to the Du family?

HAO *(hopelessly):* All right. It's our only way out.

SIYI: Ai! *(Takes a couple of steps.)*

WENCAI *(heartbroken):* Oh, Father!

JIANG *(suddenly gets up):* No, wait, wait just a minute! *(Runs into
his bedroom hurriedly.)*

(Siyi stops.)

HAO *(puzzled):* What's he up to now?

(Zhang Shun enters through the living room door.)

ZHANG: Somebody came over from the Du residence and told
me the fortune-teller insists that the coffin be moved into
their house before five o'clock tomorrow morning. They
want to ask Da Nainai if . . .

WENCAI: You . . .

(Jiang Tai rushes in again with a torn hat and a cane in his hand.)

JIANG *(to Zhang Shun excitedly):* Go and tell those bastards over
there to wait in the living room. Tell them that we're going
to pay them, and Old Master Zeng's coffin is going to stay
right here, even if we have to use it for firewood!

WENCAI: What are you . . .

JIANG *(to Zeng Hao earnestly):* Father, you just wait here. I'm going
to look up a friend of mine. *(To Wencai):* Chang Dingjai is

the Police Commissioner, and I'm sure he can help us. *(To Zeng Hao, confidently):* He's an old friend of mine. This won't be any problem for him. *(Clearheadedly):* First of all, he can talk things over with the Du family and tell them to stop stirring up trouble around here. Second, if the Dus won't budge, I can ask him to help us out. *(Condescendingly):* What's a few dollars for him? There won't be any problem here, there won't be any problem at all.

WENCAI *(almost unable to believe her own ears):* Tai, can you really do that?

JIANG *(taps his cane):* Naturally, naturally. Well, Father, I'll be going. *(Waves at Siyi.)* Da Sao, you heard me. I give you my guarantee, you take my word for it! *(Walks toward the living room door.)*

SIYI *(surprised and threatened by Jiang Tai's reassurance, feels totally at a loss):* Then Father, what about . . .

WENCAI *(happily):* Father!

(Jiang Tai takes one step into the living room, and then hurries back.)

JIANG *(holds out his hand to Wencai):* I don't have any money on me.

WENCAI *(immediately takes out a roll of banknotes from her pocket):* Here!

JIANG *(starts counting):* Thirty . . . *(Exits complacently through the living room door.)*

HAO *(confused by his action, finally manages to breathe a sigh of relief):* What's Jiang Tai up to now?

WENCAI *(fearing that others do not trust her husband, whom she has worshipped all along, says to Zeng Hao with conviction):* Don't worry, Father, he never breaks his promise. If he says he can do something, he'll do it.

HAO *(half-suspicious):* Oh!

SIYI *(unable to control her feelings):* Humph, I think he . . . *(stops herself, turns to Zeng Hao, forces a smile.)* I think things will be all right now, Father, with the coffin . . .

HAO *(seems to be soothed by this dose of hope, sighs):* Yes, we should do whatever we can. Let's just do what he says.

ZHANG (*cannot restrain his joy*): Then, Da Nainai, I'll tell them to . . .

SIYI (*her suppressed anger beginning to surface, she says harshly to Zhang Shun*): What good will that do? (*Swiftly and angrily walks toward the living room.*)

HAO (*adds hastily*): Siyi, be very nice to them. But no matter what, get them to wait just a little longer.

SIYI: All right. (*Exits through the living room door.*)

(*Zhang Shun follows and exits through the same door.*)

WENCAI (*with a happy smile*): Ruizhen, you see how crazy your uncle is? He had to wait until the last minute to . . .

RUIZHEN (*preoccupied by her own troubles*): Yes, Auntie.

HAO (*becoming more hopeful, says right after Wencai*): Ai! If we could only keep that coffin, then everything would be fine. (*Turns his head to address Zeng Ting*): Ting, do you think it's possible?

TING: Sure, Grandfather.

HAO (*nods*): Let's hope that from now on, our family fortune will change for the better . . . Yes, who knows (*Starts to get up. Ruizhen goes over to help him.*) How have you been feeling?

RUIZHEN: I'm fine, Grandfather.

HAO (*gets up, looks at Ruizhen, and then sentimentally*): Just think, you'll be a mother soon!

(*Wencai signals to Zeng Ting to go over and help his grandfather. Ting walks quietly over.*)

HAO (*looks at his grandchildren, suddenly says hopefully*): I see that you two are very happy together. From now on, the future of this family is in your hands.

WENCAI (*signals to Zeng Ting to respond*): Ting!

TING (*glances at Ruizhen before responding*): Yes, Grandfather.

HAO (*still very hopeful as he speaks to the third generation of the Zeng family*): If we can keep the coffin here, and if we don't have to sell the house, I'll go out when spring comes and see what I can do for you. For your children, I'd work like a dog! (*Wipes the corners of his eyes with a handkerchief.*) Ai, may our ancestors grant me good heatlh. And don't forget to pray diligently for me. (*Walks toward the study.*)

WENCAI (*goes over to help Zeng Hao, chiming in*): Oh yes, when spring comes, Father will be all better, Ruizhen will bring you a great-grandson, and Brother'll . . .

(*Sufang appears as the study door opens. She has just finished arranging flowers, as there are a couple of chrysanthemums in her wet hands.*)

SUFANG (*brushes the hair away from her face with her hand; says gently*): Uncle, you'd better go to your room and rest. It's all ready for you.

HAO (*happily*): Yes, yes! (*Nods to Wencai in agreement as he walks toward the study door.*) Oh yes, as soon as spring comes! . . . Ruizhen, early next spring, next spring . . .

(*Ruizhen helps Zeng Hao to the study door, looks at Sufang, turns and points secretly at the parlor. Getting the signal, Sufang nods and takes Zeng Hao's arm in her place, helping him out of the parlor. Wencai follows them. Ting is still standing in the parlor. Ruizhen glances at him, and walks quietly back from the study door.*)

RUIZHEN (*in a low voice*): Ting!

TING (*as if too afraid to look her in the eye, ruefully*): Are you leaving tomorrow morning?

RUIZHEN (*also not looking at him, says slowly but firmly in a low voice*): Yes.

TING: Are you going with the Yuans?

RUIZHEN: Yes, we're leaving together.

TING (*looks around, and puts his hand in his pocket trying to find something*): I've already written the note.

RUIZHEN (*stares at Zeng Ting*): Oh.

TING (*takes out a piece of paper, looks around again, and starts reading in a low voice*): "Miss Xie Ruizhen and Mr. Zeng Ting are hereby divorced. Married at a very young age, we are now faced with an insoluble conflict. Living together has become a hardship. The two of us hereby voluntarily dissolve the bond of . . .

RUIZHEN (*grief-stricken*): Don't read anymore.

TING (*pauses, but mindful of the procedures pertaining to this ordeal, says hesitantly):* How about our signatures, and our seals, and . . .

RUIZHEN: We'll do that in the bedroom later.

TING: All right.

RUIZHEN *(sorrowfully):* Ting, I really feel terrible for making you write this.

TING *(dumbfounded, says to her with unprecedented tenderness):* No, you've suffered enough in this family for the last two years. *(Suddenly):* Did you tell Auntie Su you decided not to have the baby?

RUIZHEN *(recollects reluctantly):* Yes! I'm even thinking of giving her back the clothing she made for the baby. Why?

TING: Oh, I figured at least one person in the family should know about it.

RUIZHEN *(concerned):* Ting, after I'm gone, what, what are you going to do?

TING: I don't know. *(In a lonely voice):* I can't go back to school now.

RUIZHEN *(very sympathetically):* Don't give up now.

TING: No, I won't.

RUIZHEN *(soothingly):* We can still write to each other all the time.

TING: All right. *(Tears start running down his cheek.)*

VOICE OF YUAN YUAN *(from outside):* Ruizhen!

RUIZHEN *(sadly):* Don't be so upset. Sometimes we have to suffer before we can really understand different things in life.

TING: That understanding is so painful sometimes!

(Yuan Yuan, whistling happily, enters through the living room door. She is wearing a knitted skirt, a thin, red pullover, and a pair of white sneakers. She looks as if she has been packing, as her hair is a bit disheveled. In one hand she holds a bird cage with the pigeon Solitude confined in it, and in the other she carries the big torn goldfish kite.)

YUAN *(loudly):* Ruizhen, my father's been looking for you all day. He wants to know whether your luggage . . .

RUIZHEN *(hushes her up immediately, smiles):* Could you lower your voice a little bit, please?

YUAN (*sticks out her tongue, then starts instantly whispering*): My Father . . . wants to know . . . whether you and your friends . . . have packed . . . your bags or not?

RUIZHEN (*prompted by Yuan Yuan's funny expression, laughs*): They're all packed.

YUAN (*still whispering*): He said . . . he can only . . . take you half-way . . . and he also asked you . . . (*Finally breathes a sigh, and recovers her usual tone.*) This is ridiculous. Why don't you come with me? My father still has a million things to ask you.

RUIZHEN (*genially*): All right, let's go.

YUAN (*instead of leaving with Ruizhen she walks up to Zeng Ting with her things, and says to him seriously*): Zeng Ting, since your father isn't here, (*raises the torn kite*) I'm giving this torn kite back to your mother. (*Sets the kite down by the table and raises the bird cage.*) And I'm giving this pigeon to Miss Su! (*Places the cage on the table.*)

TING (*nods, seems to have forgotten the feeling he had for Yuan only about a month ago*): All right.

YUAN (*to Ruizhen*): Ruizhen, let's go!

(*Pushing Ruizhen's back, Yuan Yuan ushers her out through the living room door. At the same time, Siyi enters through the same door. As they run into each other, Ruizhen looks at her mother-in-law, startled. She is then immediately pushed out of the room by Yuan Yuan, who exhorts her with a "let's go." Zeng Ting looks at them as they make their exit, and then lets out a low sigh.*)

SIYI (*turns her head and looks at them momentarily out of the corner of her eye, then walks up to Zeng Ting*): Ruizhen is hardly ever home these days. She's always out with her friends. What do you suppose she's up to?

TING (*looks at her briefly and shakes his head*): I don't know.

SIYI (*detesting her son for being so dense, but also feeling helpless about the whole matter, sighs*): Ai, my child, after all, she's your wife. I guess I should mind my own business! (*Suddenly*): Where is everybody?

TING: They've all gone to Grandfather's room.

SIYI *(complains woefully)*: Ting, did you see how badly they treated your mother just now?

(Zeng Ting looks at her briefly, then lowers his head.)

SIYI *(gets out her handkerchief)*: Your mother was destined to suffer. Your father abandoned us and ran away. It's only for your sake that I stay here and take this from them all day long. *(Wipes her tearful eyes.)*

TING: Mother, please don't cry.

SIYI *(patting Zeng Ting)*: From now on, you must tell your mother everything! *(Grumbling)*: If I hadn't found out last month that Ruizhen was pregnant, the two of you still wouldn't have told me, would you? *(Points at Zeng Ting.)* Why did you do that? *(Then suddenly becomes concerned.)* Did she take the medicine I gave her?

TING: I don't think so.

SIYI: No, I'm talking about the medicine that Dr. Luo prescribed for her pregnancy.

TING *(feels terrible inside and getting increasingly impatient)*: No, she didn't!

SIYI *(her expression changes abruptly to anger)*: Why didn't she? Tell her to take it, force her to take it! If she won't, then tell me, and I'll force it down her throat! She thinks she isn't a member of the Zeng family, but that little baby inside her belongs to us! Since she's pregnant, we let her do whatever she wants, but she's going too far! *(In a low voice)*: Ting, don't be stupid. The last few days, Ruizhen's been up to something. I don't like the look of those friends of hers *(lowers her voice even further)*. I'm worried she'll steal things from here, so I'm locking all the doors at night. You'd better be careful, I'm afraid that . . .

(Sufang enters through the study door, carrying a bowl of medicine.)

SUFANG *(gently)*: The medicine that Dr. Luo prescribed is ready now.

(Siyi glances at Sufang.)

SUFANG (*seeing that Siyi does not respond, says again*): Do you want to take it here?

SIYI (*coldly*): Leave it on the charcoal stove in my room for the time being.

(*Sufang takes the medicine, walks in front of Zeng Ting, and enters Siyi's bedroom.*)

TING (*glances at the bowl of medicine, surprised and puzzled*): Mother, how come you're taking the medicine that Dr. Luo prescribed for Ruizhen?

SIYI (*slightly embarrassed by his question at first, but quickly regains her composure; mumbles vaguely to Zeng Ting*): I, I haven't been feeling well lately (*tries to find an excuse*) and for the past few days, I've been lucky to have your Auntie Su take care of me . . . (*coughs, abruptly changing the tone of her voice*): But listen to me, my son. (*Her face darkens.*) Auntie Su is (*shakes her head*) She . . . she is really . . .

(*Sufang enters from Siyi's bedroom.*)

SUFANG: Cousin Siyi, Uncle's looking for you!

SIYI (*nods indifferently, then turns to Ting*): Ting, come with me.

(*Ting follows Siyi and they exit through the study door. It is getting even darker outside. The honking of geese can be heard from outside as they sweep desolately across the darkening late autumn sky. Sufang looks a bit tired as she sighs softly. Suddenly she sees the bird cage on the table, picks it up and stares at the caged pigeon inside. At this time, Ruizhen enters, carrying a rattan trunk stuffed with infant clothing. She lays the basket softly on the other small table, and approaches Sufang quietly.*)

RUIZHEN (*in a low voice*): Auntie Su!

SUFANG (*startled, turns to her*): You're here! (*Puts down the cage.*)

RUIZHEN: Have you read the long letter that I left in your room?

SUFANG (*nods*): Yes.

RUIZHEN: Are you angry at me?

SUFANG (*smiles woefully but kindly*): No . . . (*Suddenly*): Do you really have to leave?

RUIZHEN (*unwilling to part with her, says sadly*): Yes.

SUFANG (*sighs, not trying to dissuade her, but actually distressed by her imminent departure*): Don't go!

RUIZHEN (*suddenly getting emotional*): Auntie Su, are you asking me to go on living like this?

SUFANG (*seems to be reminiscing about something; speaks slowly as a gleam of determination appears in her eyes*): I understand, there comes a time when you just cannot take it any longer.

RUIZHEN (*there is a spark of expectation in her eyes as she grasps Sufang's pale fingers*): Then, how about you?

SUFANG (*looks at Ruizhen sorrowfully; says quietly*): Ruizhen, let's not talk about it. After you leave, I'll be even more lonely. Maybe from then on I won't have to speak at all, I'll be even more . . .

RUIZHEN (*grasps her hand even tighter, gently urges her to sit down*): No, no, Auntie Su, you can't act like this, you can't be like this for the rest of your life! (*Imploring her anxiously*): Auntie Su, I have to leave soon, so why can't you be frank with me. Why can't you tell me your . . . (*Sufang's big eyes shine with tears in the dimming twilight, but she manages to suppress an outburst.*)

SUFANG (*slowly*): What do you want me to say?

RUIZHEN (*hesitantly*): You, for instance, you, you . . . (*Suddenly*): why don't you leave this place?

SUFANG (*lonely*): Where can I go?

RUIZHEN (*excitedly*): There're so many places you can go. First of all, you can come with us.

SUFANG (*shakes her head*): No, I can't.

RUIZHEN (*sits next to her, intimately*): Did you read the book I gave you?

SUFANG: Yes.

RUIZHEN: Do you think that it's right?

SUFANG: Yes.

RUIZHEN (*smiles*): Then why don't you leave with us?

SUFANG (*softly but firmly*): I can't!

RUIZHEN: Why not?

SUFANG *(looks at her):* I just can't!

RUIZHEN *(urgently):* But why?

(Sufang is about to speak, but again shakes her head.)

RUIZHEN: At least you can give me a reason!

SUFANG *(with great difficulty):* I feel that . . . I have some unfinished business here.

RUIZHEN: I don't understand.

SUFANG *(smiles, and stands up):* Never mind. You don't have to understand. I don't think I could explain anyway.

RUIZHEN *(pressing her, directly):* But why don't you go and find him?

SUFANG *(a bit uneasy):* You mean . . .

RUIZHEN *(straightforward):* Find him, go and find Father!

SUFANG *(calms down, and contemplates):* Why should I?

RUIZHEN: Don't you love him?

(Sufang lowers her head.)

RUIZHEN *(pressing on):* Then why don't you want to look for him? Why don't you? *(Very directly):* Auntie Su, I'm not as foolish as I used to be. A month ago, I wouldn't have asked you these questions. I suppose you could tell then that I knew what was going on. *(Sorrowfully):* I have to leave soon. There's no one here but you and I. Auntie Su, please tell me, why don't you go find him, why don't you?

SUFANG *(sighs):* Do you think he and I can be happy just by meeting again?

RUIZHEN *(rebutting):* Are you happy here?

SUFANG: At least I, I can take care of . . . *(Suddenly becomes tongue-tied.)*

RUIZHEN *(anxiously):* Go on, Auntie Su, you told me once that some day we would have a heart-to-heart talk.

SUFANG: I, I'll tell you . . . *(A beautiful glow gradually appears on her face, as her pale cheeks begin turning rosy. Her voice trembles with emotion.)* Since he's gone, I am taking care of his father and watching over his children. I'm taking care of the calligraphy and paintings that he treasures and feeding the pigeons that he loves. Even the people whom he dislikes, I feel I should be kind to them, like them, love them, because . . .

RUIZHEN (*interrupts, still pressuring her*): But why?

SUFANG (*pauses, but has not changed her tone; moved*): Because at least they were close to him, even if he didn't love them. (*Breathless and elated, even she herself is startled by the realization of this long-repressed emotion which has surfaced in words.*)

RUIZHEN (*draws her breath*): So you gave up your whole life to take care of someone like Ting's mother, my mother-in-law, and watch over her.

SUFANG (*smiles bitterly*): With your father gone, don't you think she needs a little support?

RUIZHEN: Really Auntie Su, can you forget the way she treated you in the past, and even now, the way she . . .

SUFANG (*woefully but also sympathetically*): Do we have to remember all that unhappiness? If it's for him, for him alone, for his . . .

RUIZHEN (*cannot bear listening any longer*): Oh, my dear Auntie, you're so devoted. But why can't you devote yourself to something more important? Why can't you just forget about him? Why surrender yourself to such a worthless nobody, such a worthless . . .

SUFANG (*as if something has pierced her heart*): Don't talk about your father like that.

RUIZHEN (*defending herself*): Didn't Grandfather say the same things about him?

SUFANG (*agonizing*): No, don't talk like that. Nobody understands him.

RUIZHEN (*lets out a sigh; then, mournfully*): Then you mean you'll never see him again?

(*Sufang lowers her head slowly.*)

RUIZHEN (*sincerely*): Tell me, Auntie Su!

SUFANG (*almost inaudible*): Yes.

RUIZHEN: Why did you let him go?

SUFANG *(as if reminiscing):* I, I could see he was suffering here, I felt sorry for him.

RUIZHEN *(questions her):* Now that he's gone, are you happy?

SUFANG *(softly):* Hmm.

RUIZHEN *(sighs):* Oh, how can the two of you go on living like this?

SUFANG *(a smile sweeps gently across her face):* Wouldn't you be happy if someone you cared for were happy?

RUIZHEN *(with great concern, slowly):* Then you don't miss him here?

(Sufang lowers her head.)

RUIZHEN: And doesn't he miss you?

(Tears start to run silently down Sufang's pale cheeks.)

RUIZHEN: So for the rest of your life, you'll be all alone . . . how can the two of you go on suffering like this?

SUFANG *(staring into space):* Suffering, maybe, but not all alone.

RUIZHEN *(deeply moved):* My poor Auntie Su, I know, I understand. I understand now! But I'm afraid. Maybe Father'll come back one of these days. And when he comes back, everything will be the same as before: we'll still be suffering, holding onto what little we have left, staring into space and hoping for who knows what. We'll all suffocate here, and no one will . . .

SUFANG *(trembles, but suddenly shakes her head with determination):* No, he'll never come back again.

RUIZHEN *(stubbornly):* But suppose he does?

SUFANG *(wipes away the tears from the corners of her eyes):* He won't, he'd rather die than come back here to live. *(Stares at the moistened handkerchief as she lowers her head, slowly and softly.)* He already came back once.

RUIZHEN *(shocked):* He came back here without letting anybody know?

SUFANG: Yes.

RUIZHEN *(surprised):* When?

SUFANG: The day after he left.

RUIZHEN *(still a little shocked by the news, breathes a deep sigh)*: Oh!

SUFANG: He said he wanted to be somebody, and that he'll never come back even if he is dying. *(So emotional that she is unable to prevent herself from rambling on uncharacteristically.)* He said he had been a horrible son to his father, a bad father to his son. And he mentioned you over and over again. He told me to take care of everything: his family, his paintings, his pigeons. Finally he started crying. He also said . . . he also said that the person he really cared about the most is . . . *(smiles behind her tearful eyes)*. Ruizhen, he's just like a child. It's so hard to believe he's almost a grandfather.

RUIZHEN *(sternly)*: So from now on you're going to take care of the family for him?

(The following questions and answers follow without a pause.)

SUFANG *(calmly)*: Yes.

RUIZHEN *(pressing on)*: And you'll follow our dying grandfather around all day long?

SUFANG *(nods)*: Yes.

RUIZHEN: And take care of his son?

SUFANG *(looks at Ruizhen, frowns a little)*: Yes.

RUIZHEN: And wait on the whole family?

SUFANG *(stubbornly)*: Yes.

RUIZHEN *(slightly annoyed)*: And put up with my mother-in-law every single day?

SUFANG *(shudders slightly)*: Uh! . . . Yes.

RUIZHEN *(pressing her)*: And take her abuse?

(Sufang stares fixedly).

RUIZHEN *(pressing even harder)*: And keep on taking it like that?

SUFANG *(still staring)*: Yes.

RUIZHEN *(heatedly)*: For the rest of your life? *(Pounding on every word)*: Until you die?

SUFANG *(lowers her head and rubs her forehead; replies slowly)*: Until I die!

RUIZHEN *(explodes, and sorrowfully)*: But my dear Auntie Su, why do you have to do this?

SUFANG *(raises her head):* For . . .

RUIZHEN *(interrogating her):* Yes, for . . .

SUFANG *(with difficulty):* For . . . I don't know how to say this . . . *(suddenly a beautiful smile appears on her face)* for . . . the sake of living my life.

RUIZHEN *(forcing a question):* You really think that Father'll never come back?

SUFANG *(smiles):* Will the sky collapse?

RUIZHEN: You've really made up your mind to stay here in the Zeng family for the rest of your life? In this prison? All for this one dream, this fantasy of yours, all for one person . . .

SUFANG *(gently):* Perhaps I'll leave one day . . .

RUIZHEN *(anxiously):* When?

SUFANG *(smiles):* It'll be the day the sky falls, when the deaf-mutes begin to speak!

RUIZHEN *(commiserating):* Auntie Su, giving up your own happiness for the sake of one person is dangerous; there's no reason to do that. *(Emotionally):* I was a fool once, but Auntie, you're still . . .

(The room is gradually growing darker. The crows flutter over the eaves of the house, announce their presence, and then fly away. As Ruizhen speaks, the soldier's bugle from the city wall can be heard echoing intermittently in the desolate night air. The bugle call continues until the curtain closes at the end of scene 1.)

SUFANG: Ruizhen, let's not talk about it. *(Suddenly raises her head and looks out.)* Listen, what's that?

RUIZHEN *(knows that Sufang is unwilling to continue the conversation):* Oh, it's the bugle from the city wall.

SUFANG *(listens attentively):* It's so sad!

RUIZHEN *(nods):* Yes, it's getting dark out. When I was alone in my room I used to hate that sound. It made everything so gloomy!

SUFANG *(tearfully):* It sounds so sad! *(Suddenly grasps Ruizhen's hand affectionately, and says softly):* But Ruizhen, suddenly I feel so happy! *(Rubs her chest gently.)* My heart is so warm!

It feels as if spring is here! *(Excited.)* Isn't this what life is all about? Just days and days full of sadness and happiness. *(Cries.)* Sometimes it makes you want to cry, and sometimes it makes you want to laugh!

RUIZHEN *(takes out a handkerchief and dries Sufang's tears; calls to her in a low voice):* Auntie Su, why are you crying again? Auntie Su, are you . . .

SUFANG *(listens to the distant bugle):* Don't mind me, just let me cry! *(Still with tearful eyes, forces out a smile.)* But I'm really smiling! Ruizhen . . . *(Ruizhen lowers her head sadly, covering her nose with her handkerchief.)* Ruizhen, you don't have to cry for me! *(Tenderly):* Even though I'm sad inside, I am crying because I'm really very happy!

(Ruizhen raises her head and looks at Sufang momentarily, then starts sobbing. Sufang rubs Ruizhen's hands, then in a soft voice that reflects a mixture of happiness and sorrow, begins to console her.)

SUFANG: Don't cry, Ruizhen, I haven't talked so much for I don't know how many years. Now I feel that my heart is opening up, and the sun is warming it for me. Ruizhen, you're so nice! If it weren't for you, I wouldn't be so happy now; if it weren't for you, I wouldn't have been able to talk about him so much, and so warmly. *(Even more excitedly):* Ruizhen, if you think you can be happy out in the world, then go on, go out there! I'll still be happy here. Don't cry, Ruizhen. You think this is a prison? It isn't, it really isn't . . .

RUIZHEN *(sobbing):* No, no, Auntie Su, I really feel sorry for you! I'm afraid! Don't get so excited. Oh, your face is burning again, I'm afraid . . .

SUFANG *(imploring):* Ruizhen, don't pay any attention to me! I've never felt so happy before! *(Walks over to the table where Ruizhen has put her trunk.)* Ruizhen, why don't you take this box of baby clothes with you. *(Ruefully):* After you leave, you should do your best to help others! Give the good ones away, and keep the rest for yourself. We should help whoever's in need. The purpose of life is much more than just looking out for ourselves. *(Opens the trunk.)* If you don't need this clothing anymore, give it to the children who have nothing to wear. *(Suddenly pulls out a red cotton cape.)* Do you like this cape?

RUIZHEN: Yes, it's very pretty.

SUFANG *(cheerfully pulls out a small white cap):* Isn't this cute?

RUIZHEN: Yes, it really is.

SUFANG *(happily pulls out another item: a small green silk dress):* How about this one?

RUIZHEN *(also happily):* That's really beautiful!

SUFANG *(blithely as her face glows with a beautiful tenderness):* No, this is nothing! There's another one here . . . *(Giggles, lowers her head, and starts rummaging through the trunk.)*

(The sound of the mournful bugle floats incessantly into the parlor. At this moment the living room door opens, slowly and gently. In the dimming twilight, Zeng Wenqing appears. He is thinner and paler and looks very tired. A worn lined gown covers his frail body as he shuffles into the parlor, head lowered, with a scroll painting under one arm. Sufang has her back to him and continues rummaging through the trunk with her head lowered. Ruizhen faces the door.)

RUIZHEN *(sees Wenqing and cries out as if she is having a nightmare):* Oh, my God . . .

(Sufang is elated as she raises with both hands a big, beautiful stuffed doll with black hair and bright eyes, which is wrapped in a piece of red silk swaddling cloth. She smiles broadly and looks expectantly at Ruizhen.)

SUFANG: Look! *(Suddenly detects the changed expression on Ruizhen's pale and nervous face.)* Who is it?

RUIZHEN *(stares dully):* I think, the sky . . . the sky is falling. *(Suddenly covers her face with her hands.)*

SUFANG *(turns and sees Wenqing as he hesitates; he looks toward them but it is as if he cannot see them clearly):* Oh!

(Wenqing immediately lowers his head and quietly walks straight into his bedroom. Right after he enters his room, Siyi enters, running through the study door.)

SIYI *(excited and happy):* Is Wenqing back?
SUFANG *(dumbfounded):* He is back!
(Siyi immediately runs into her own bedroom. Sufang stands there, frozen. The sound of the distant bugle through the lonely night air.)

Slow curtain

Scene 2

About ten hours after act 3, scene 1, it is the darkest period before dawn. A kerosene lamp turned to its brightest setting lights up the whole parlor. The torn goldfish kite has disappeared, but the pigeon cage still sits on the table. The pigeon is sleeping peacefully, with its head nestled under a wing. It is very cold in the parlor. At this time of night, only the warmest clothes can ward off the chill of the late-autumn air. A strong west wind is swirling outside, stirring through the aspen trees in the garden and causing them to moan as if they were being battered by rain. As the ravaged trees prompt our sorrow and inspire loneliness, the torn paper windows flap in the wind. The night watchman's distant gong can be heard occasionally. The howling wind brings every now and then the strained voice of the old peddler who sells noodle cakes in the long, dark alley outside. In the temperamental wind his voice quivers, fades out, and becomes audible again.

The night is one of the most agonizing in the history of the Zeng family. Most of them have not gone to bed. The ailing Old Master, Zeng Hao, has hardly slept. All night he has been sitting and brooding over the imminent removal of his precious coffin, the one lacquered over and over again for so many years. Realizing that in a few hours he will have to relinquish this treasure to others, he suffers worse pain than if he were being burned alive.

The Du family has insisted that the coffin be moved before five o'clock in the morning. They have been advised that the "coffin welcoming" ceremony must take place no later than the end of the "yin" hour, that is, five in the morning. In the meantime, Jiang Tai, who left the previous evening to negotiate for a loan, has still not returned. Zeng Wencai has been running around frantically trying to locate her husband, and at the same time attempting to console her disheartened father. She has telephoned around and sent out messengers, but Jiang Tai is not to be found. Seeing how much the Old Master is suffering, the rest of the family feels obliged to keep him company. Naturally, some of them sincerely hope that Jiang Tai will come back with the money, so that they can drive away the inconsiderate Du family messengers. Others voice the same hope, but are actually worried that if Jiang Tai returns with a loan, their chances of making a handsome profit will be jeopardized. This same evening, other family members are packing busily, both shedding tears and rejoicing over their departure. Mournful and hopeful at the same time, they reminisce about the past and long for the future—the future that belongs to the Peking Man of tomorrow and has nothing to do with those who spend most of their lives in coffins.

In this cold, desolate parlor, Wenqing sits, motionless, on the sofa, as if in a daze. He has changed into a worn, dark-gray quilted silk gown. With his hands drawn into the long sleeves of his gown, he sits and stares into space. From his eyes, the arch of his brows, and the corners of his lips, we detect weariness, despair, and boredom. He listens glumly to the distant gong, to the sound of the wind and the leaves, and is barely stirred intermittently by the incessant chatter of Siyi beside him.

Siyi is wearing a light-blue linen quilted gown. She has been talking constantly and now seems worn out as she awaits Wenqing's reply. Holding a bowl of medicine in one hand and an empty bowl in the other, she pours the medicine from one bowl into the other in order to cool it. Finally, she drinks the medicine in one gulp and picks up another bowl of water to rinse out the bitter taste in her mouth.

SIYI *(puts down the bowl and starts speaking again):* All right, you're back now, at least no one in the Zeng family can blame me anymore. *(Grins sarcastically.)* It just shows how wrong your dear sister was, that I didn't force her brother to stay away from this family and never return.

(Wenqing raises his head and looks at her wearily.)

SIYI *(glances at Wenqing out of the corner of her eye; appears to be sincere):* So, what do you think? . . . Well, in that case, I take it that you agree? *(Then looks as if she does not understand.)*

Why aren't you saying anything? I'm not forcing you into this!

WENQING *(sighs, helplessly):* What, what are you going to do this time?

SIYI *(wide-eyed, she appears indignant at the injustice done her):* I don't know what I can do to please you. *(With a determined expression):* As far as I'm concerned, I think I've done everything I could to be nice! Only today, your brother-in-law humiliated me in front of your father and my children; and for your sake, I put up with him! I also went to see your Su Meimei just now, and tried my best to invite her over here, so that we can discuss the matter, and talk things over together . . .

WENQING *(growing increasingly impatient with her haggling, finally raises his head and asks):* To talk about what?

SIYI: Talk about what? To talk about what we've been discussing, of course! *(Feeling sure of Wenqing's intention, says sarcastically):* This isn't child's play. Don't be like a child who really wants candy but is too shy to ask for it. I'm a straightforward person, I'll always say what's on my mind. I don't like men who want to eat mutton but can't stand the smell.

WENQING *(wearily):* It's almost daybreak. Why don't you go to bed!

SIYI *(without acknowledging what he said, continues in the same tone):* I told your sister all about it just awhile ago . . .

WENQING *(shocked):* What, you even told my sister . . .

SIYI *(scowls at Wenqing):* Why? Why shouldn't I tell her? . . .

(Wencai enters through the study door. She is wearing the flannel gown from before, but this time she has also put on a brown sweater. Not having slept all night long, she looks exhausted and her hair is a bit disheveled.)

WENCAI *(brushing her hair with her fingers in an attempt to tidy it a bit):* Why Brother, it's almost five o'clock and you're still up?

WENQING *(forces a smile):* Oh, yes.

WENCAI *(turns to Siyi; asks anxiously):* Is Jiang Tai back yet?

SIYI: No.

WENCAI: I thought I heard someone opening the front gate just now.

SIYI *(coldly):* That must have been the coffin-bearers sent over by the Du family to move the coffin.

WENCAI: Ai! *(The chill of disappointment gradually penetrates her heart. She shivers and curls up on the old sofa.)* Oh, it's so cold!

SIYI *(listens attentively, says deliberately):* Listen, they're locking the gate again! *(Brings up the matter again.)* Well, what do you think? *(Smiling, though she addresses Wencai somewhat stiffly.)* Sister, about the matter I was just discussing with you . . .

WENCAI *(still perturbed, at a loss):* What?

SIYI *(glances over at Wenqing coyly):* About Su Meimei marrying into the family.

WENCAI *(remembers, but knowing that Siyi is scheming again, says with an uneasy smile):* Well, don't you think it's rather inappropriate?

SIYI *(very forthright):* What's inappropriate about it? *(Then affectionately):* My dear sister, don't go on thinking that my heart is *(raises her little finger)* no bigger than the head of a pin. I'm not the kind of woman who needs a husband around all day long. I can never be "virtuous" no matter how hard I try, but I still have a little generosity left in me. *(Very humbly):* Actually, it's not a matter of generosity, it's simply a cousin marrying another cousin. That can only draw the family closer together. It's natural and it happens all the time.

WENCAI *(earnestly):* No, I still think that we should talk to Cousin Su about it first.

SIYI *(laughs unsympathetically):* Why? How can she refuse? I'm an honest person, so I'll be frank with you. I'm not the only one who knows what's on her mind. After all, Cousin Su is really a good person, we can't ignore that. So *(sincerely to*

Wenqing), "my dear cousin," it's now your turn to speak your mind. Since Gu Nainai's here now, I want you to give me your honest opinion right in front of her.

(Wenqing glances over at Wencai, then lowers his head and remains silent.)

SIYI *(pressing him):* Tell me everything so that I can make all the preparations for you!

WENCAI *(seems to realize her brother's predicament; speaks in his behalf):* I don't think this is such a good idea.

SIYI *(rolls her eyes):* Why not? Don't worry, my dear sister, I could never mistreat Cousin Su. This can only draw us closer together than ever before! *(Tries even harder to show her generosity.)* I'm a very straightforward person. Late last night, I was going through some of the jewelry I brought with me to the Zeng family. And what a coincidence, the first thing I saw was this elegant pair of pearls. I decided I'm going to give them to Cousin Su as an engagement present from Wenqing. *(As she speaks, she picks up a pair of old pearls that were removed from a hairpin, and hands them over to Wencai.)* Now, what do you think?

WENCAI *(reluctantly takes the pearls from her, and praises with studied politeness):* They are quite nice.

SIYI *(becomes even more talkative):* You know how impatient I am, I've even found a place for the two of them to live. The moment the Yuans step on that train, I'm going to send for the plasterers. If everybody chips in and helps, I can guarantee you a wedding feast in no time. I've got just about everything ready . . . *(Looks at Wenqing with an expression of blended mockery and praise.)* Our Wenqing's so kind and considerate, he's worried that his Cousin Su won't get the proper treatment. I've already told myself that, from now on *(goes ahead and talks to her heart's content)*, well, this may sound vulgar but from now on, there're going to be two bosses in this house. *(Laughs vulgarly.)* And neither will mistreat the other!

WENCAI (*full of anxiety, but forced to laugh nervously with her*): Oh
yes, but don't you think we ought to consult Father first?
(*Zhang Shun enters through the study door. With sleepy eyes, he looks
like someone has just gotten him out of bed. He is still not dressed
properly.*)
ZHANG (*calls out as he enters the parlor*): Da Nainai!
SIYI (*without paying any attention to Zhang Shun, pretends that she
has not heard Wencai clearly*): What?
WENCAI: I said we should consult Father first.
SIYI (*very confidently*): Hai, with such a nice daughter-in-law (*insinuating*) to take care of him, doesn't it make the whole
situation more "official"? (*Suddenly*): But there's only one
thing. I don't care how people address her at home. But in
front of strangers, she'll still be "Miss Su." If we call her
"Nainai" or "Mrs. Zeng," people will laugh at us . . . (*turns
and glances at Wenqing*). Actually, I don't really care, but
Wenqing insisted. It's his idea. (*Wenqing is about to respond,
but she suddenly turns to Zhang Shun*): What's the matter,
Zhang Shun?
ZHANG: The Old Master wants to see you.
SIYI: You mean he still hasn't gone to bed?
ZHANG: No . . .
SIYI (*to Zhang Shun*): All right, let's go. Hai! (*Exits hurriedly through
the study door.*)
(*Zhang Shun follows her and exits.*)
WENCAI (*watches Siyi leave, stands up and walks over to Wenqing,
and slowly consoles him*): You haven't eaten anything yet, have
you?
(*Wenqing looks at Wencai, shakes his head, and hopelessly stares into
space.*)
WENCAI: Let me go and get you some date biscuits.
WENQING (*waves his hand impatiently*): No, no, no (*then again wear-
ily*), I can't eat anything now.
WENCAI: Then come into my room and freshen up a bit, and lie
down for awhile.

WENQING (*still absentmindedly*): No, I don't want to go to sleep.

WENCAI (*hesitates, but finally asks*): Why . . . why isn't she letting you into the bedroom tonight?

WENQING (*smiles bitterly*): Humph, she wants me to apologize to her.

WENCAI: Well, did you?

WENQING (*hopelessly but firmly*): Of course not! (*Closes his eyes again.*)

WENCAI (*sympathetically but helpless*): Ai, whoever heard of such a thing! Her husband has just come back, and within two minutes, she's back to her old ways again.

(*A strong west wind is still howling outside. Chen Naima enters through the study door. Following a whole night of exhaustion, she is pale and her eyes appear sunken. She enters, yawning, wearing a quilted jacket.*)

CHEN (*sees that Wenqing has his head lowered and his eyes closed, she imagines he is sleeping; she turns to Wencai and speaks in a low voice*): Is Master Wenqing sleeping?

WENCAI (*also softly*): I don't think so.

(*Chen Naima walks up close to Wenqing, who still has his eyes closed, unwilling to speak.*)

CHEN (*looks at Wenqing, and shakes her head sympathetically, then turns to Wencai and says compassionately in a low voice*): I think he's asleep. (*Sighs softly, takes off her jacket, and covers Wenqing with it.*)

WENCAI (*still softly, but anxiously*): No, no, you'll catch a cold. I'll go and get . . . (*Walks toward her bedroom.*)

CHEN (*stops Wencai, and says anxiously in a hoarse voice*): I'm fine. It's all right, Gu Xiaojie, you'd better go and check on the Old Master.

WENCAI (*worried*): What's the matter?

CHEN (*painfully*): We tried to get him to lie down for awhile, but he just wouldn't do it. He's so restless. He sits down and gets up, and sits down again. All he cares about is whether Gu Laoye is back or not.

WENCAI *(heartbroken):* What are we going to do? What are we going to do? There hasn't been a word from him all night, God knows where he . . .

CHEN *(shakes her head):* Ai, what a pity! *(Then not wanting to wake Wenqing, moves Wencai away from where he is sitting.)* Isn't this awful? Earlier today he promised his coffin to someone; now in the middle of the night, he suddenly realizes that he's giving away that old thing he's been keeping so many years . . . just imagine, wouldn't you be upset! Wouldn't you . . .

(Zhang Shun enters through the study door.)

ZHANG: Gu Nainai!

(Chen Naima immediately points at Wenqing, who looks as if he is sound asleep, waving at Zhang Shun and signaling him to be quiet.)

ZHANG *(instantly lowers his voice):* The Old Master would like to see you.

WENCAI: Ai! *(Takes a couple of steps and turns.)* Where's Miss Su?

CHEN: She just finished massaging the Old Master's legs . . . She's probably cleaning up in her room.

(Wencai follows Zhang Shun out the study door. The wind begins to subside; but the fallen leaves are still being blown about the front yard, making light chafing sounds. The sound of the night watchman's gong fades into the distance, and finally disappears. The hoarse voice of the old noodle cake peddler is heard from the alley again. Chen Naima yawns, and walks up to Wenqing.)

CHEN *(lowers her head and looks at Wenqing; seeing that he still has his eyes closed, she calls, softly and lovingly):* My poor Master Wenqing!

(Wenqing opens his eyes, which still have that hopeless, weary look. He props himself up on his arms.)

CHEN *(startled):* Master Wenqing, you're awake?

WENQING *(as if awakened from a sickly drowsiness, raises his head slowly):* Oh, it's you, Naima!

CHEN *(rubs the corners of her eyes as she looks at Wenqing):* Yes, it's me, my Master Wenqing! *(Looks at him again and shakes her head, saying fondly):* My poor dear, you've gotten even skinnier! Why are you sleeping out here?

WENQING *(mumbling):* Hmm, Naima.

CHEN: Ai, my Master Wenqing, it must have been so awful for you out there! *(Dries her tears again.)* Miss Su and I missed you every single minute. Poor Miss Su . . .WENQING *(suddenly grasps Chen Naima's hand firmly):* Naima, oh my dear Naima!

CHEN *(heartbroken):* Oh my master, my dear Master Wenqing! Have, have you seen Miss Su since you've been back?

WENQING *(cannot reply to her; can only grasp her dry and wrinkled hand):* Naima! Naima!

CHEN *(aware of his deepest feelings, says affectionately):* I've already asked her to come here.

WENQING *(shocked, and very emotionally):* No, no, Naima!

CHEN: Oh, my Master Wenqing! How could anyone ever know that you're about to become a grandfather! Master Wenqing!

WENQING *(perturbed):* No, no, don't let her come here! Why do you have to . . .

CHEN *(watches the study door):* Don't, don't, maybe it's her!

(Sufang enters through the study door. She has changed into a black woolen "qi pao" dress which attractively sets off her long black hair, pale complexion, and calm expression. Her large eyes gently suggest sorrow and fatigue. She enters the room softly like a beautiful spirit. Wenqing stands up, deeply moved.)

SUFANG: Chen Naima!

CHEN *(purposely tries to appear casual):* Oh, Miss Su, you're still up?

SUFANG: Yes. *(Cannot find anything to say.)* I, I'm here to see how the pigeon is doing. *(Walks toward the table where the pigeon cage is.)*

CHEN *(casually):* Yes, go ahead! *(Suddenly remembers something.)* I'd better go see if Young Master Ting and his wife are up. Da Nainai asked the two of them to see the Yuans off. *(Walks toward the study as she speaks.)*

WENQING (*picks up her quilted jacket; in a low voice*): Naima, your jacket!

CHEN: Oh! Oh! My jacket (*smiles at them*), you see how poor my memory is getting. (*Takes the jacket, and exits through the study door, mumbling something.*)

(*It is still a short while before dawn. The wind is gradually becoming stronger, and the aspen trees shake with the sounds of heavy rain. In the distance, the first cockcrow can be heard echoing in the wind. Wenqing and Sufang face each other in silence. Not a word is spoken. Wenqing lowers his head, and starts walking slowly toward his bedroom.*)

SUFANG (*finally takes her eyes off the pigeon cage*): Wenqing!

(*Wenqing stops, but is still afraid to turn and look at Sufang.*)

SUFANG: Naima told me that you're looking for me.

(*Wenqing turns around, slowly raises his head, and looks at Sufang. Sufang looks back.*)

WENQING: Sufang! (*Lowers his head again.*)

(*Sufang unconsciously turns and stares at the caged pigeon.*)

WENQING (*searching for something to say, mournfully*): The, the pigeon's still here.

SUFANG (*calmly*): Because it can't fly anymore!

WENQING (*startled and dumbfounded*): I . . . (*Suddenly realizes the implication, covers his face, and starts sobbing.*)

SUFANG: Wenqing.

(*Wenqing is still weeping.*)

SUFANG (*knitting her brows*): Don't. Why must you cry?

WENQING (*weeps bitterly, as he throws himself on the sofa*): Why did I come back! Why did I come back! I knew I shouldn't, but why did I come back!

SUFANG: You couldn't fly anymore, so you came back.

WENQING (*sobs as he voices his grief*): No, no, you don't understand . . . out there . . . out there in that stormy world . . .

SUFANG: Wenqing! (*Takes out a key and hands it to Wenqing.*)

WENQING: Eh?

SUFANG: This is the key to the trunk!

WENQING (*puzzled*): What?

SUFANG (*quietly*): All your paintings are in that trunk. (*Puts the key on the table.*)

WENQING (*shocked and helpless*): What's the matter, Sufang?

(*Momentary silence. From outside, the sound of the wind and the leaves.*)

SUFANG: It's so windy out there!

(*Through the sound of the wind blowing, calls of* "Auntie Su! Auntie Su!" *can be heard from outside.*)

SUFANG (*listens attentively*): Is there someone calling me?

WENQING (*also listens, but cannot hear*): No, I don't think so.

SUFANG (*very firmly but calmly*): Yes, there is!

(*Siyi enters through the study door.*)

SIYI (*to Sufang, half-sarcastically and half-innocently*): Oh! I just knew that you'd be here! (*Affectionately*): Oh Su Meimei, my back's hurting me again. Could you come and massage me a little? Please? I forgot to tell you. When your Cousin Wenqing came back, he brought you a very nice present.

WENQING (*extremely embarrassed*): You . . .

SIYI (*ignoring him, she picks up the pair of pearls from the table and hands them to Sufang*): Look at the pearls. Look how big and round they are!

WENQING: Siyi!

(*Zhang Shun enters through the study door, and seeing that they are talking, stops abruptly.*)

SIYI (*simultaneously laughs, ignoring Wenqing*): Your Cousin Wenqing said that he wanted to give this to you as a . . .

WENQING (*trembling with rage, suddenly bursts out in anger*): How can you be so wretched? (*Instantly runs into his bedroom.*)

SIYI: Wenqing!

(*He slams the bedroom door shut.*)

SIYI (*her face darkens as she says coldly*): Ai, I really don't know how to please this husband of mine!

ZHANG (*walks up to her; in a low voice*): Da Naimai, the Dus' housekeeper said that it's already past five o'clock, so we better move the coffin over there now.

SIYI: All right, I'll be right there.

(Zhang Shun exits through the living room door.)

SIYI *(abruptly)*: Well, Su Meimei, we'll talk later. *(Starts for the study door, then turns around, smiles, and says very affectionately)*: You know, my stomach's bothering me again, could you please go to the kitchen and make a hot salt compress for me.

(Sufang lowers her head. Siyi exits through the study door. Sufang stares at the pigeon. The sound of a gust from outside. Ruizhen enters through the living room door.)

RUIZHEN: Auntie Su!

SUFANG *(without moving)*: Yes.

RUIZHEN *(urgently)*: Auntie Su!

SUFANG *(turns to Ruizhen slowly)*: Ruizhen, you're right, this place is really a prison!

RUIZHEN *(startled, suddenly grasps Sufang's hand firmly)*: Oh my God! The deaf-mutes are beginning to speak! *(Excitedly)*: It's getting late, Auntie Su, let's go.

SUFANG *(ruefully and softly)*: Can I really walk out through this door?

RUIZHEN: We're supposed to see Mr. Yuan off, but we'll get on the same train. I'm sure that he'll understand.

VOICE OF SIYI *(from outside)*: Su Meimei! Su Meimei!

RUIZHEN: She's coming! *(Hides behind the living room door.)*

(Siyi immediately enters through the study door.)

SIYI: Oh, you're still here all by yourself! Father wants his ginseng soup right now. Let's go.

(Sufang nods in agreement, and is about to make her exit.)

SIYI *(suddenly becomes affectionate)*: Oh, Cousin Su, I just remembered something. I think I may as well talk to you now. *(Suddenly spots Ruizhen.)* What are you doing in there?

(Ruizhen simply stares at her.)

SIYI: What are you staring at, you good-for-nothing? Have you gotten your husband up yet?

RUIZHEN: I have.

SIYI: Make sure that he has enough to wear when he goes to see the Yuans off. *(Glances at Ruizhen in disgust; then to Sufang):* Let's talk in the side room. *(Drags Sufang along as she exits through the study door.)*

(Yuan Rengan enters through the living room door, wearing a heavy coat.)

RUIZHEN: Mr. Yuan.

MR. YUAN *(smiling):* Well, are you leaving with us?

RUIZHEN *(suppresses her own excitement):* Yes, Auntie Su's things are all packed in your trunk. We've sent it ahead already.

MR. YUAN *(surprised):* Oh! . . . you've finally talked her into it, eh?

RUIZHEN *(nods):* Yes, she's leaving with me.

MR. YUAN *(understands partially, but still finds it incredible):* Hmm, where are you two going to go?

RUIZHEN: Mr. Yuan . . . *(Looks a bit distressed.)*

MR. YUAN: All right, you don't have to tell me. *(Sincerely):* But I hope there's someone to take care of you along the way.

RUIZHEN: Yes, there will be.

MR. YUAN: That's fine. We'll leave in twenty minutes.

(He goes back to the living room. Sufang enters simultaneously through the study door.)

RUIZHEN *(runs over to her happily):* Auntie Su! Auntie Su . . . *(Suddenly sees Sufang's dreadfully pale face.)* How come you're so pale? What happened? What did she say to you?

SUFANG *(mournfully):* Yes, I know I must leave this place.

(A sudden uproar of gongs, drums, and oboes can be heard from outside. It is so loud that it dwarfs the sound of the wind.)

RUIZHEN *(startled, turns):* What's that?

SUFANG: It must be the Du family's "welcoming party" for the coffin.

RUIZHEN: Forget about that, let's go.

SUFANG *(woefully):* No, you go first.

RUIZHEN *(surprised):* Why aren't you . . .?

SUFANG: I'll be there in a minute. I just want to see him one last time.

RUIZHEN *(a bit annoyed):* See who?

SUFANG *(sorrowfully):* My poor Uncle!

RUIZHEN *(finally understands):* Oh! *(Also a little sad.)* All right, I'll go ahead and wait for you at the front gate.

VOICE OF WENCAI *(from outside):* Jiang Tai! Jiang Tai!

(Ruizhen exits immediately through the living room door. Sufang takes a few steps toward the study as Wencai enters tearfully through the study door.)

WENCAI *(anxiously):* Is Jiang Tai back?

SUFANG: I don't think so.

WENCAI: Where can he be at this hour? *(As she speaks, she falls on the sofa and starts sobbing.)* Oh my father, my poor father!

SUFANG *(also anxiously):* What's the matter?

WENCAI *(dries her tears with a handkerchief and complains):* The Dus are insisting that the coffin be moved over there right away, but Father wouldn't allow it. The pathetic old man is clinging to his coffin for dear life just like a little child. I just couldn't bear to look at him! *(Raises her head, and looks at a very mournful Sufang.)* Cousin, please go ask him to come in here. It's too much watching him hold on to that coffin!

(Sufang walks sorrowfully toward the study door; she exits through the same door.)

WENCAI *(at the same time, to herself):* Father, Father, what good are children like us? *(Rises, unable to restrain herself).* Brother! Brother! *(Walks toward Wenqing's bedroom.)* What's the use of people like us? What good are we?

(The deafening sound of firecrackers is heard from outside. Wencai stops and turns. Zhang·Shun enters through the study door, somewhat tearfully.)

WENCAI: What's that?

ZHANG *(annoyed and sad):* The Dus are setting off firecrackers to welcome the coffin! They're moving it now. We've opened the back gate for them to bring it through.

(Amid the sound of firecrackers, we hear the well-paced steps and the low and heavy voices of the bearers murmuring "Ai-ho, Ai-ho" carrying out the coffin. Mixed with this are the voices of the housekeepers of the Du family, shouting their instructions. Outside the study window the lights of numerous wobbling lanterns move back and forth with their bearers. At this moment, Zeng Hao, supported by Chen Naima and Sufang, enters through the study door. He is white as a sheet; his eyes are badly bloodshot. Having suffered through such a traumatic experience, he is almost delirious, and refuses to enter the parlor despite vigorous exhortations. Chen Naima, busily drying her own tears, is relentlessly trying to console him and at the same time to drag him into the parlor. Sufang looks at Zeng Hao sorrowfully. Siyi follows behind them. She is wiping the corners of her eyes with a handkerchief. Of course, we cannot tell whether she is really drying tears or if something has gotten into her eyes.)

CHEN *(repeatedly):* Come on in, Old Master . . . It's no use looking anymore! Come in now . . .

HAO *(turns and yells hoarsely):* Wait, wait! Tell them to wait just a little longer! Tell them to wait! *(Turns to Siyi, wobbling; speaks incoherently.)* Go tell them that the money's coming, he's coming back soon, he's going to bring the money back soon! Wait! Ask them to wait!

SUFANG: Uncle! you . . .

(Sufang helps Zeng Hao to sit down. Seeing that the old man is gasping in his agitation, she suddenly recalls something she can get for him and immediately hurries through the study door.)

CHEN *(still consoling):* Let them go, Old Master *(struck with abhorrence).* Let them put their corpse in it!

HAO *(almost begging):* Siyi, please go talk to them!

SIYI *(cannot help feeling a little sorry for the old man; helpless, she tries to console him the way an adult would treat a child):* Don't worry, Father! When we get the money, we'll buy you another one.

HAO *(furious):* Wencai, you go talk to them! Go talk to them now! *(Stamps his foot.)* Is Jiang Tai coming back?

WENCAI *(pained by this fiasco all along, says repeatedly):* He is, Father! Oh, he'll be back!

(The sound of firecrackers is getting louder. The coffin-bearers are ap-proaching as their footsteps get louder and louder. They get so close that one can almost feel them passing by.)

HAO *(shouts)*: Jiang Tai! Jiang Tai! *(To both Wencai and himself)*: Where is he! Where is he!

(The living room door is thrown open all of a sudden. His face red as a beet, Jiang Tai staggers into the parlor. His hair is disheveled and his clothes are wrinkled. The sound of firecrackers gradually subsides.)

HAO *(almost cannot believe his own eyes)*: Jiang Tai, you're finally back!

JIANG *(like a clown, his facial expression shows both laughter and sor-row, complacency and dejection; he nods to Zeng Hao and mum-bles)*: I . . . am . . . back!

HAO *(overwhelmed by joy)*: Oh, good, you've come back at just the right time! Zhang Shun, tell them to wait! Give them the money, and tell them to get out! Zhang Shun, go ahead.

(Zhang Shun immediately exits through the study door.)

WENCAI *(simultaneously walks up to Jiang Tai)*: Where, where is the money you borrowed? *(Holds out her hand.)*

JIANG *(claps his hands once, happily and excitedly)*: It's right here! *(Takes a roll of toilet paper out of his pocket, and slams it onto Wencai's palm.)* Take it!

WENCAI: You, you're . . .

JIANG *(turns toward the door at the same time)*: Get in here! Get the hell over here!

(Sure enough, it is a policeman who enters through the living room door. He is followed by a very embarrassed Zeng Ting, who is carrying a half-full bottle of brandy.)

JIANG *(still staggering, but very self-righteous)*: That's him! *(Points to the policeman, speaks very clearly.)* He . . . is . . . the one! *(Turns to the rest and starts defending himself.)* I checked into a room at the Peking Hotel, and spent the night there. And today they said I stole something. They said I stole some-thing from them . . .

HAO: What? . . .

POLICEMAN *(knowingly):* Excuse me, but this gentleman has had the great inconvenience of spending a night at our station.

JIANG: You liar! I stayed at the Peking Hotel!

POLICEMAN *(still very politely):* He was at our station!

JIANG *(irate):* Peking Hotel! *(Points at the policeman.)* Look, your commissioner's a good friend of mine! *(Staggers around the parlor as he speaks; his anger has suddenly and totally vanished.)* Here, this is my family! And this is my wife! *(Forgets totally about his quarrel with the policeman; starts getting carried away.)* And this is my father-in-law, Mr. Zeng Hao! *(Raises his head suddenly, and laughs.)* Look! *(Points at his bedroom.)* That's my bedroom! *(Looks at the policeman, still laughing, and starts mumbling and acting as if he were a tourist guide.)* This is my table! *(And walks up to the door of his bedroom.)* And this, my door! *(He staggers into his bedroom, still mumbling.)* And this is my . . .

(A soft, abrupt "thud" can be heard from Jiang Tai's bedroom.)

WENCAI: Tai, you . . . *(Runs into her bedroom.)*

POLICEMAN: Ladies and gentlemen, you can see for yourselves that I've done my best to escort the Young Master home safely. *(Gives a casual salute to the people in the parlor and exits through the living room door.)*

VOICES OF MEN OUTSIDE *(excited):* Move it out!

(A roar of laughter can be heard, followed immediately by low and heavy footsteps. Zeng Hao again turns around abruptly.)

CHEN: What are you doing?

HAO: I want a look . . . one last look . . .

CHEN: Forget about it, Old Master . . .

(Zeng Hao walks toward the study; Chen Naima hurries over to help him. At the same time, Siyi also goes over to help. Chen Naima and Zeng Hao exit through the study door. The noise and footsteps from outside gradually become more remote and finally subside.)

SIYI *(helps Zeng Hao to the study door, then comes back to Zeng Ting; curiously):* Ting, what did that policeman say?

TING: He said that Uncle was very drunk and went shopping in a store where they sell imported things, and stole a bottle of brandy when he was there.

SIYI: Did they catch him red-handed?

TING: Yes, and somehow he managed to finish half the bottle at the police station. And for some strange reason he even admitted stealing it. This *(raises the half-empty bottle)*, this is what's left! *(Sets the bottle on the table and then sits down on the sofa with an expresion of pain on his face.)*

SIYI *(rejoicing in Jiang Tai's misfortune)*: Good! Well, your uncle has finally learned a trade! *(Walks toward her bedroom.)* Wenqing *(reaches the door)*, Wenqing, I was talking to your Su Meimei just now, and I think she's pretty happy about it. It'll be so nice from now on. You'll be all settled down, and so will I. You can enjoy her company whenever you want; and after I have my baby, someone will be there to take care of me!

TING *(his mother's last sentence pierces his ears like a needle; shocked, he jerks his head up)*: What did you say, Mother?

SIYI *(surprised by his question)*: What . . .

TING *(rises slowly)*: You said you're also . . . eh . . .

SIYI *(a little embarrassed)*: Yes? . . .

TING *(fearfully)*: Having a baby?

SIYI *(her expression confirms Zeng Ting's fear)*: Well?

TING *(looks hopelessly at his mother; after a moment of silence, he says, pounding on every word)*: Ai! Go ahead and do whatever you want! *(Suddenly runs out through the living room door.)*

SIYI: Ting! *(Wants to run after him, but stops after a couple of steps.)* Ting! *(Painfully)*: My little Ting!

(Wencai enters hastily from her bedroom.)

WENCAI: Where's Father?

TING *(stupefied)*: He went to say goodbye to his coffin.

(Just as Wencai is about to walk toward the study door, Chen Naima enters through it, supporting Zeng Hao. Zeng Hao stands by the door refusing to move. He is looking toward the outside, shouting. Wencai quickly runs up to the door. The light of the lanterns fades quickly as the bearers march away into the distance.)

HAO (*still facing the outside, shouts at the bearers in the distance*): No, don't! Don't do that! They're not carrying it properly!

CHEN (*simultaneously*): Forget about it, Old Master, please!

WENCAI (*incessantly*): Father! Father!

HAO (*as the coffin is moved further away, Zeng Hao, still attached to it, points and shouts*): Oh, no, not that way! You can't knock it around like that! (*To Chen Naima*): Go tell them to stop bumping it into the wall like that! That coffin's got Sichuan varnish on it! It can't be knocked around like that! It can't take it!

SIYI: Now just let it go, Father. What they do to it is their business.

HAO (*having been reminded of the cruel reality by Siyi, he suddenly quiets down and stares into space; after a moment of silence, he suddenly bursts into tears*): Oh my wife! My dear wife! You're lucky you died so long ago. And here I am, an old man who's letting his very own coffin be . . . (*stamps his foot.*) What's the use of staying alive and having children! What's the use of having so many rotten children around! (*Painfully throws himself on the sofa.*)

(*Suddenly part of the mud wall collapses with a loud noise. All are silent.*)

WENCAI (*in a low voice*): The wall just collapsed.

(*During the momentary silence, Jiang Tai staggers in again from his bedroom.*)

JIANG (*with good intentions, says to Siyi in a very friendly manner*): Da Sao, I've been telling you, I've been warning you ever since the Midautumn Festival that it's going to collapse! Collapse! Tell me now, was I right or not!

(*Siyi glances at him in disgust, turns around abruptly, and exits through the study door.*)

JIANG (*shakes his head*): Ai, nobody wants to listen to me! Nobody pays any attention to me! Nobody! (*While he is speaking, he picks up the bottle of brandy and reenters his bedroom.*)

WENCAI (*anxiously*): Jiang Tai! (*Follows him into the bedroom.*)

(The cock crows again in the distance.)

CHEN: Ai!

(At this time, the whimpering voices of women can be heard coming faintly from next door. Sufang enters through the study door with a bowl of ginseng soup in one hand and a blanket hanging over her other arm. The blanket is actually intended for her forthcoming journey.)

HAO *(raises his head)*: Who's crying?

CHEN: I suppose Old Master Du has breathed his last; let me go check.

(Zeng Hao lowers his head again. Chen Naima hurries out through the study door. The cock crows.)

SUFANG *(walks up to Zeng Hao and says softly)*: Uncle!

HAO *(raises his head)*: Eh?

SUFANG *(tenderly)*: Your ginseng soup. *(Hands it to him.)*

HAO: Oh, did I ask for it?

SUFANG: Yes! *(Places it in Zeng Hao's palm.)*

(Suddenly, Yuan Yuan enters very quietly through the living room door. She is still wearing the same clothes; but this time she has on in addition a jacket the same color as her skirt. A black silk scarf with white dots is tied loosely around her neck.)

YUAN *(stands at the door and says anxiously in a low voice)*: It's late, hurry up!

SUFANG *(nods)*: Hmm.

(Yuan Yuan smiles and withdraws to the living room, closing the door behind her. Hao takes a sip, puts the bowl down on the end table next to the sofa, and then sighs weakly but deeply.)

HAO: Ai! *(Lowers his head and shuts his eyes.)*

SUFANG *(concerned)*: Are you feeling better?

HAO *(faintly)*: Yes, yes . . .

SUFANG *(commiseratively)*: Uncle! I'm leaving now!

HAO *(nods)*: Yes, go rest for awhile.

SUFANG: Ai *(says slowly)*, I'm going away now!

HAO *(absolutely exhausted; feebly)*: Yes!

(Sufang turns around and takes a couple of steps. Then she turns her head and takes another look at the pathetic old man. She is unable to

walk away without squeezing out her last drop of care for him, covering him gently with the blanket she was going to take with her.)

HAO *(mumbles suddenly)*: Come back later!

SUFANG *(tearfully)*: Yes, I'll be back. *(Stares at Zeng Hao, walking backwards.)*

HAO *(still with his eyes shut)*: And you'll give me a good rubdown.

SUFANG *(tears running down her cheeks)*: Yes, I'll give you a good one! A good one! . . . I'll give . . .

(She seems to hear someone entering the parlor; immediately turns toward the living room and exits there. The moment Sufang steps out, Wencai enters from her bedroom.)

WENCAI *(sees that Zeng Hao is dozing off, says to him softly)*: Father, your ginseng soup's getting cold!

HAO: No, I don't want it now.

WENCAI *(comforting him sadly)*: Father, don't be so sad! Everything will be all right, no matter what happens. *(Sheds tears.)* Just wait, Father. Next spring, you'll feel much better, your great-grandson will be born, Jiang Tai'll turn over a new leaf and Brother'll find a good job for himself . . .

(Suddenly a low groan from Wenqing's bedroom, and then the sound of someone falling out of bed.)

WENCAI *(frightened)*: Oh! *(Turns to Zeng Hao.)* Father, I'll go look. *(Pushes into Wenqing's bedroom.)*

(Chen Naima enters through the study door.)

HAO *(weakly)*: Old Master Du . . . Is he dead?

CHEN: He's dead, it's all over now.

HAO: Oh, my eyes hurt so! Will you turn the lamp down for me please?

(Chen Naima turns down the kerosene lamp, dimming the whole parlor. The light of dawn slowly filters through the closed folding doors of the living room. Wencai reenters, running nervously through Wenqing's bedroom door.)

WENCAI *(anxiously, in a low voice)*: Chen Naima, Chen Naima!

CHEN: Oh!

WENCAI *(horrified, in a strained voice)*: Don't scream. Go get Da

Nainai, tell her that my brother just swallowed opium. His pulse has stopped.

CHEN *(frightened):* Oh! *(About to weep.)*

WENCAI *(restraining her):* Please don't cry, Naima, I don't think the Old Master could take it at this point. Hurry up and tell her!

(Chen Naima runs out the study door.)

WENCAI *(forcing herself to be calm, walks over to Zeng Hao):* Father, the sun's coming up now, let me help you in to bed.

HAO *(gets up, and takes a couple of steps):* What was that in the bedroom just now?

WENCAI *(mournfully):* A rat. The place is crawling with rats.

HAO: Oh.

(Zen Hao walks slowly toward the living room door, with the help of Wencai. A cock crows again. Morning has broken. A mule cart rolls slowly down the long lane. In the distance, a train whistles sharply to signal its departure.)

Slow curtain